DISEASES & DISORDERS

Meningitis

D0002302

Meningitis

Titles in the Diseases and Disorders series include:

DISEASES & DISORDERS

Meningitis

John F. Grabowski

LUCENT BOOKS

An imprint of Thomson Gale, a part of The Thomson Corporation

THOMSON
™
GALE

Detroit • New York • San Francisco • New Haven, Conn. • Waterville, Maine • London

On cover: A woman in Niger, Africa, is vaccinated against meningitis.

LIBRARY OF CONGRESS CATALOGING-IN-PUBLICATION DATA

Grabowski, John F.
   Meningitis / by John F. Grabowski.
      p. cm. — (Diseases and disorders series)
   Includes bibliographical references and index.
Contents: What is meningitis?—A medical emergency—Preventing meningitis—A lifetime of consequences—Meningitis and the future.
      ISBN-13: 978-1-59018-411-0 (hardcover : alk. paper)
      ISBN-10: 1-59018-411-4 (hardcover : alk. paper)
   1. Meningitis—Juvenile literature. I. Title. II. Series: Diseases and disorders series.
RC376.G73 2006
616.8'2—dc22
                                                          2005035477

Printed in the United States of America

Table of Contents

"The Most Difficult Puzzles Ever Devised"

Charles Best, one of the pioneers in the search for a cure for diabetes, once explained what it is about medical research that intrigued him so. "It's not just the gratification of knowing one is helping people," he confided, "although that probably is a more heroic and selfless motivation. Those feelings may enter in, but truly, what I find best is the feeling of going toe to toe with nature, of trying to solve the most difficult puzzles ever devised. The answers are there somewhere, those keys that will solve the puzzle and make the patient well. But how will those keys be found?"

Since the dawn of civilization, nothing has so puzzled people—and often frightened them, as well—as the onset of illness in a body or mind that had seemed healthy before. A seizure, the inability of a heart to pump, the sudden deterioration of muscle tone in a small child—being unable to reverse such conditions or even to understand why they occur was unspeakably frustrating to healers. Even before there were names for such conditions, even before they were understood at all, each was a reminder of how complex the human body was, and how vulnerable.

While our grappling with understanding diseases has been frustrating at times, it has also provided some of humankind's most heroic accomplishments. Alexander Fleming's accidental discovery in 1928 of a mold that could be turned into penicillin has resulted in the saving of untold millions of lives. The isolation of the enzyme insulin has reversed what was once a death sentence for anyone with diabetes. There have been great strides in combating conditions for which there is not yet a cure, too. Medicines can help AIDS patients live longer, diagnostic tools such as mammography and ultrasounds can help doctors find tumors while they are treatable, and laser surgery techniques have made the most intricate, minute operations routine.

This "toe-to-toe" competition with diseases and disorders is even more remarkable when seen in a historical continuum. An astonishing amount of progress has been made in a very short time. Just two hundred years ago, the existence of germs as a cause of some diseases was unknown. In fact, it was less than 150 years ago that a British surgeon named Joseph Lister had difficulty persuading his fellow doctors that washing their hands before delivering a baby might increase the chances of a healthy delivery (especially if they had just attended to a diseased patient)!

Each book in Lucent's Diseases and Disorders series explores a disease or disorder and the knowledge that has been accumulated (or discarded) by doctors through the years. Each book also examines the tools used for pinpointing a diagnosis, as well as the various means that are used to treat or cure a disease. Finally, new ideas are presented—techniques or medicines that may be on the horizon.

Frustration and disappointment are still part of medicine, for not every disease or condition can be cured or prevented. But the limitations of knowledge are being pushed outward constantly; the "most difficult puzzles ever devised" are finding challengers every day.

A Global Threat

Few things are as frightening to a patient and his or her family as a diagnosis of bacterial meningitis. From the time of its recognition in 1805 through the early twentieth century, the disease was nearly always fatal. Although it can strike anyone at any age, infants and young adults are especially at risk. Said Dr. John P. Quinn: "What is striking about meningitis is that it can be so devastating. It typically infects young, previously healthy people. Although the number of cases is small nationally, each case is very dramatic."[1]

Making the disease even more terrifying is the fact that it strikes with such swiftness. Reports Dr. James Turner of the University of Virginia, "It's the only infectious disease that I'm aware of that can take an otherwise healthy individual, and within four or five hours they're hospitalized, in an intensive care unit, in shock, on a ventilator, clinging to life."[2]

One form of the disease, known as meningococcal meningitis, is particularly terrifying due to its potential for causing large-scale epidemics. This affliction brings added misery to some of the world's neediest people. A region in sub-Saharan Africa extending from Senegal in the west to Ethiopia in the east is known as the "meningitis belt." In this region of eighteen countries and over 350 million people, infection rates are approximately one per ten thousand people. During epidemics, this rate can jump as high as one per one hundred people.

Fortunately, medicine has made great strides in its bid to conquer meningitis. The introduction of antibiotics has made the forms of meningitis caused by bacteria curable if diagnosed and treated at an early stage. Moreover, globally it does not kill as many people as tuberculosis, malaria, and human immunodeficiency virus (HIV). Still, it remains a major cause of death and disability and is therefore one of the most serious infectious diseases affecting the world's population. Even in years when there are no epidemics, a million cases are estimated to occur worldwide; each year, approximately two hundred thousand of those struck down by the disease die.

While the incidence of meningitis is far higher in the nonindustrialized nations of the world, new vaccines have greatly reduced the mortality rate of bacterial meningitis in industrialized countries. In the United States, the disease strikes about twenty thousand Americans each year and is fatal in approximately three hundred cases. Approximately 20 percent of those who survive suffer some sort of long-term consequences.

New Worries

In addition, a new form of the disease has appeared. Since the mid-1990s, the incidence of meningitis occurring on college campuses has risen sharply. Why this has happened mystifies

A baby is hospitalized with meningitis, a disease for which infants and young adults are particularly at risk.

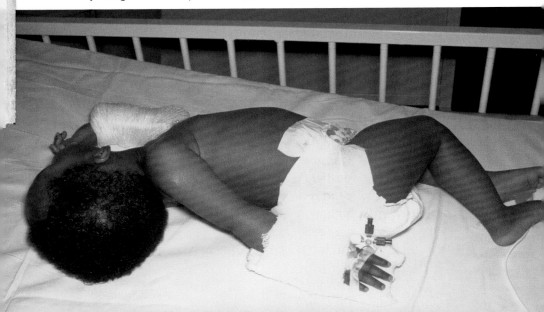

experts. Says Turner, "One possibility is perhaps a different strain of the bacteria has been introduced into the population. . . . This may be a strain that simply has new characteristics that people's immune systems simply have never seen before. Or maybe it's a strain that is particularly virulent or powerful. It's not really clear."[3]

In the United States, approximately 100 to 125 college students contract the disease each year, and 5 to 15 die from it. What particularly saddens the victims' loved ones is that up to 80 percent of those cases could well have been prevented by vaccination. "I can't tell you how much it hurt," said one mother about her stricken son, "to know that he didn't have to die."[4]

Through the efforts of modern medicine, progress has been made in the battle to bring meningitis under control. Much remains to be done, however, to conquer this dreaded disease and to bring an end to the pain and suffering that it has brought to so many families around the world.

CHAPTER ONE

What Is Meningitis?

Twenty-two year old Nicki was a vibrant, happy, fun-loving young college student. One week, while fighting a cold, she went out with a group of her friends on a Saturday night to help relieve the stress of final exams. The next morning, she had a headache, a sore throat, and a temperature of 100.8°F. (38.2°C). Nicki refused to see a doctor, however, believing she just had a case of the flu.

By that afternoon, Nicki had begun vomiting and having diarrhea, but she still did not do anything about it. Her boyfriend finally called her parents to say that she was much worse. They immediately rushed her to a hospital.

After examining Nicki, the doctor told her parents he suspected meningitis. He ordered a spinal tap done and began treating her with penicillin. Unfortunately, his efforts were for naught. Nicki's condition deteriorated rapidly. She died just six hours after reaching the hospital and less than fifteen hours after the onset of the symptoms of the disease.

Attacking the Central Nervous System

Meningitis is an inflammation of the meninges, the membranes that surround the brain and spinal cord, which together comprise the central nervous system. Most often the inflammation is caused by one of several types of bacteria. Regardless of which of these microbes causes meningitis, the involvement of the brain makes the disease dangerous, and as Nicki's case illustrates, potentially fatal.

The Meninges

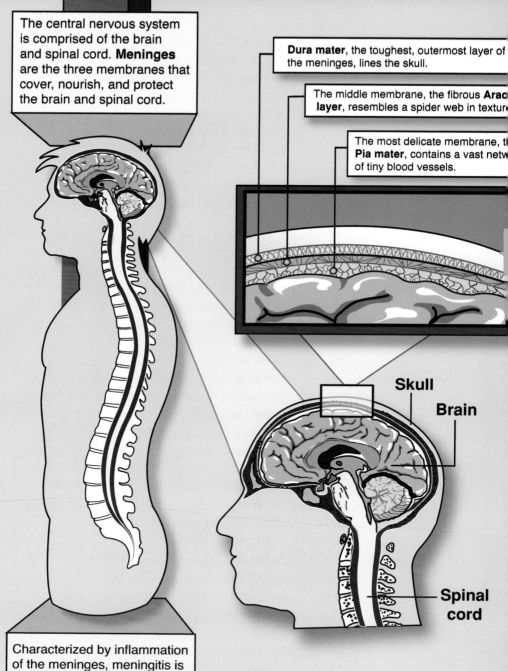

The central nervous system is comprised of the brain and spinal cord. **Meninges** are the three membranes that cover, nourish, and protect the brain and spinal cord.

Dura mater, the toughest, outermost layer of the meninges, lines the skull.

The middle membrane, the fibrous **Arac layer**, resembles a spider web in texture

The most delicate membrane, t **Pia mater**, contains a vast netw of tiny blood vessels.

Skull

Brain

Spinal cord

Characterized by inflammation of the meninges, meningitis is a disease caused by certain bacteria, viruses, and fungi.

In Ages Past

Meningitis is nothing new. Clinical symptoms of the disease were documented during the Middle Ages, although it was not recognized as a distinct disease. Prior to the nineteenth century, in fact, meningitis was lumped together with two other diseases, encephalitis and typhus, under the general term "brain fever." Although doctors could describe symptoms, they had no idea where in the brain the infection was located.

The English physician Thomas Willis (in 1661) was probably the first to describe an outbreak of bacterial meningitis. However, a Swiss physician named Gaspard Vieusseux is usually credited with giving the first clear account of the disease. In describing the outbreak that swept through Geneva, Switzerland, in 1805, Vieusseux wrote:

> At the end of January in a family composed of a woman and three children, two of the children were attacked and died in less than forty-eight hours. Fifteen days later the disease appeared in another family in the neighbourhood composed of a father, mother and five infants, four of whom were attacked almost at the same time, and all died from the tenth to the twelfth of February, after having been sick fourteen to fifteen hours with striking symptoms of malignancy. . . . One did not realize how much these rapid and numerous deaths could produce terror, although we did not doubt that there was a malignant contagious fever against which one should take the greatest precautions. As a consequence all the furniture and clothing of the two families were burned.[5]

Dr. Thomas Willis encountered bacterial meningitis in England in 1661.

Meningitis and Encephalitis: What Is the Difference?

Meningitis and encephalitis are serious inflammations of the nervous system with many similarities. While meningitis is an inflammation of the meninges surrounding the brain and spinal cord, encephalitis is an inflammation of the brain itself. In both cases, the disease is usually brought on by an infection, which can be either bacterial or viral.

Many of the symptoms of meningitis and encephalitis are similar. In both instances, the disease starts fairly abruptly. Fever is usually present, and patients complain of pain in the head, neck, or both. The main difference is found in the individual's mental state. Since encephalitis involves an infection of the brain itself, the patient often shows some sign of altered brain function. This may include confusion, disorientation, or a lessening of alertness. The meningitis patient is initially alert, with no such loss of command of mental processes.

Unfortunately, Vieusseux did not know what caused the disease that was responsible for the reported thirty-three deaths, and he was unable to treat it. The disease came to be referred to as cerebrospinal fever.

The following year, a pair of Massachusetts doctors gave a vivid description of the symptoms of the first stages of meningitis in a letter to the editor of the *Medical and Agricultural Register*. Wrote L. Danielson and E. Mann:

> Without any apparent previous predisposition, the patient is suddenly taken with violent pain in the head and stomach, succeeded by cold chills, and followed by nausea and puking . . . respirations short and laborious; tongue a little white toward the root . . . the eyes have a wild vacant stare . . . the heat of the skin soon becomes much increased . . . these symptoms are accompanied by a pecu-

liar fearfulness . . . and continue from six to nine hours when coma (suppression of sense and voluntary motion) commences . . . the extremities become cold; livid spots . . . appear under the skin, on the face, neck, and extremities; pulse small, irregular, and unequal; spasms occur at intervals, which increase in violence and frequency in proportion as the force of the circulation decreases.[6]

In time, scientists learned that the site of the infection was the meninges, which are a series of three membranes that encase the brain and spinal cord. The pia mater, or pia, is the innermost layer, composed mostly of capillaries, or tiny blood vessels. These capillaries cling to the brain and spinal cord like a fine mesh. The arachnoid layer surrounds the pia mater; the space between this layer and the pia mater contains the cerebrospinal fluid that helps cushion the brain when the head receives a jolt. The final, outermost layer, known as the dura mater, or dura, is tough and shiny. It lies closest to the inside of the skull and restricts the movement of the brain within the bony structure. Still, the exact cause of the inflammation that is meningitis remained a mystery.

Beginning to Understand

It was not until 1887 that *Neisseria meningitidis*, the bacterium that causes the most dangerous form of meningitis, was identified by the Viennese doctor Anton Weichselbaum. Weichselbaum observed the organism in the cerebrospinal fluid of a young patient who had died of the disease. He then isolated the meningococcal (from the Greek *meningo* meaning "membrane" and *coccal* meaning "grain" or "seed") bacteria in the cerebrospinal fluid of several other patients suffering from the same symptoms.

Researchers have since learned that although it is the cerebrospinal fluid that becomes infected with the bacteria, viruses, or other microbes associated with meningitis, it is the resulting inflammation that produces many of the symptoms of meningitis. Like any inflamed tissue, the brain tissue swells, forcing it against the interior of the skull. "Inflammation in the brain is dangerous," says Victor Nizet, an associate professor of pediatrics at the University of California at San Diego. "While other parts of the body can afford swelling with minor ill effect, the brain cannot. There's no place to expand, and swelling causes blood vessels to compress, cutting off oxygen to cells."[7]

An artist illustrates *Neisseria meningitidis* bacteria attacking the meninges of the brain.

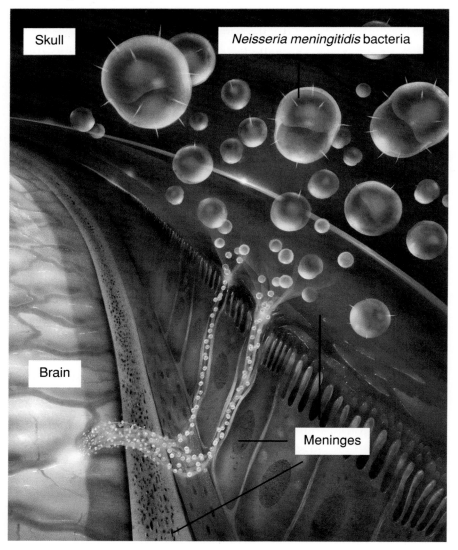

Skull

Neisseria meningitidis bacteria

Brain

Meninges

Infection may also damage the brain another way. To remain healthy, brain cells must maintain a delicate balance of substances, including oxygen, carbon dioxide, glucose, calcium, sodium, and potassium. If this balance is upset in any way, such as by infection, the brain cells may be deprived of nutrients they require or be exposed to substances that are toxic. The resulting damage to the cells may be irreparable.

One puzzling aspect of meningitis is how the microbes that cause the disease manage to infect the cerebrospinal fluid to begin with. Because the brain is susceptible to damage from toxic substances, the cells lining the capillaries of the brain are designed to prevent many agents of infection from passing from the bloodstream into the brain tissue. This is known as the blood-brain barrier. One of the questions facing doctors is why the barrier does not block the germs that cause meningitis. Says Kelly Doran, assistant adjunct professor of pediatrics at the University of California at San Diego, "It's been important to figure out how some of these bacteria have developed the ability to get in there."[8]

Solving the mystery of how infectious agents get past the blood-brain barrier is a key goal for scientists, since the majority of meningitis infections are contracted this way. Other means of infection are better understood. Infections, for example, may be acquired when an infectious agent spreads from infected tissue close to the meninges, such as that in the ear or sinuses. Skull fractures also provide a pathway by which organisms can reach the meninges and cause infection. Certain surgical procedures in which tubes are inserted in the skull in order to drain excessive amounts of cerebrospinal fluid also increase the risk of meningitis being contracted.

The least common route by which infectious agents can reach the meninges is called intraneural spread. In this method, an organism enters the body a distance away from the head and spreads along a nerve. The nerve becomes a kind of ladder to the skull, where the organism can eventually multiply and cause meningitis. The herpes simplex virus, which occasionally causes viral meningitis, is known to spread in this fashion.

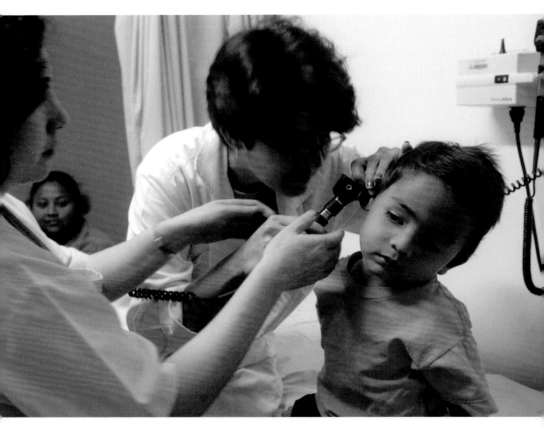

A doctor performs an ear exam. Since the meninges are near the ears, meningitis may be contracted through an ear infection.

Bacterial Meningitis

The types of agents that pass through the blood-brain barrier and cause meningitis vary widely, but the most common organisms to cause life-threatening symptoms are bacteria.

Bacteria are microscopic, single-celled organisms. Among the most primitive forms of life on earth, bacteria come in three basic shapes: rod- or stick-shaped (bacilli), sphere-shaped (cocci), and helical- or spiral-shaped (spirilla). Those that cause meningitis are usually spherical. Various bacteria can cause meningitis, but two of the most frequent culprits are meningococci and pneumococci. As these terms suggest, both organisms are spherical in shape.

The Most Common Victims

Meningococcal meningitis is caused by a bacterium known formally as *Neisseria meningitidis*. There are twelve different types of *Neisseria meningitidis*. Five strains, known as serogroups A, B, C, Y, and W135, can cause meningitis. In its various forms meningococcal meningitis most commonly strikes children. No matter what its victim's age, however, *Neisseria meningitidis* wreaks havoc as it releases potent endotoxins, or poisons, that cause extensive cell damage.

As serious as the disease it causes is, the *Neisseria meningitidis* bacterium is fairly common. It normally lives in the lining

In India, a young patient ill with bacterial meningitis receives an injection from her doctor.

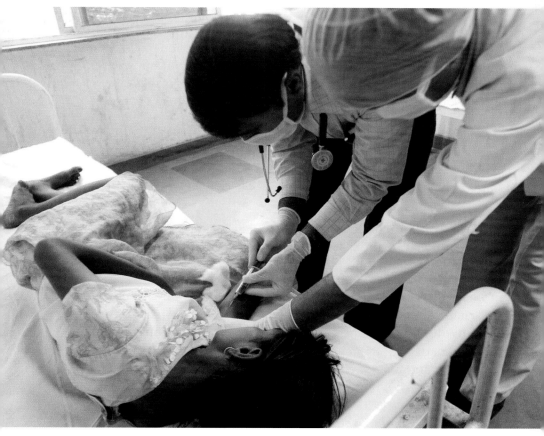

of the nose and throat known as the mucosa. Under circumstances that researchers have yet to completely understand, the bacteria can pass through the mucosa. At this point, it enters the bloodstream. Ordinarily, the blood-brain barrier prevents the bacteria from moving from the bloodstream to the cerebrospinal fluid. Sometimes, however—again for reasons that scientists are still trying to unravel—that barrier breaks down, and the meninges are vulnerable.

A Deadly Complication

Meningitis caused by *Neisseria meningitidis* is a serious illness, although the great majority of individuals who contract it recover. This form of meningitis, however, sometimes occurs in conjunction with an often-fatal infection known as meningococcal septicemia.

Once the meningococcal bacteria have entered the bloodstream, any weakening of the body's immune system can allow the bacteria to reproduce uncontrollably. In the normal course of their life cycle, the bacteria die, and as they do they break down and release poisons. These endotoxins can cause blood vessels to rupture. This often causes individuals to develop what is called a purpuric rash, which can quickly spread. As the hemorrhaging continues, the victim's blood pressure drops to dangerously low levels. The toxins can also cause blockages in blood vessels, leading to tissue death resulting in the loss of fingers, toes, or even entire limbs.

The way in which the meningococcal bacteria attack the body was described in the *Nova* television program titled "Killer Disease on Campus":

> Every meningococcal bacterium is surrounded by a slimy outer coat that contains a poisonous chemical called an endotoxin. As the bacteria multiply and move through the bloodstream, they shed bubbles that contain concentrated amounts of toxin. They also act as decoys, confusing the body's immune system. The endotoxin targets the heart, affecting its ability to pump, and also causes blood vessels throughout the body to leak. As every vessel starts

to hemorrhage, major organs like the lungs and kidneys are damaged and eventually destroyed.[9]

Meningococcal septicemia affects more than twenty-five hundred people a year in the United States. Approximately 12 percent of those who contract the disease die from it. Although antibiotics can usually kill the bacteria easily, they cannot destroy the bubbles containing the lethal endotoxins. The result can be massive damage:

> As soon as the bacteria enter the bloodstream, unleashing poisonous endotoxin, the body responds. White blood cells, the hunter-killers of the immune system, lock on to the bacteria. They engulf the bacteria, coming into contact with the endotoxin. The poison causes the white cells to release chemicals that make the blood vessel walls

One symptom of meningococcal septicemia, a rash beneath the skin, mottles this patient's legs.

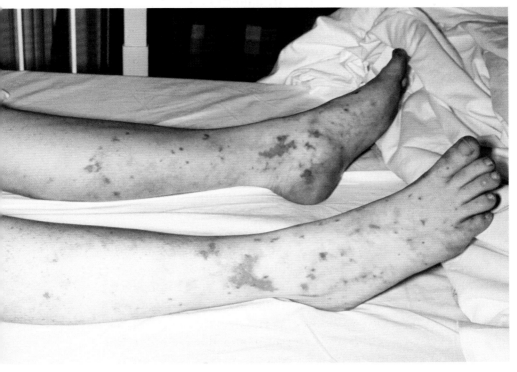

sticky. The white cells then become trapped on the walls, leaving a trail of damage.

Gradually, the lining of the blood vessels is stripped away, and as the damage increases, the vessel walls break up, and pieces fall off. The blood's repair cells, called platelets, rush to plug up the damaged areas. Dangerous clots begin to form. The proteins that normally prevent clotting have all been destroyed.

Within minutes the small blood vessels of the body are completely blocked. The damaged blood vessels disintegrate, and blood and other fluids hemorrhage into the surrounding tissue. It is this cascade of events that causes the distinctive rash that appears beneath the skin, and kills tissue throughout the body.[10]

Meningitis in Adults

Whereas meningococcal meningitis is most common in children, pneumococcal meningitis is the most common form of the disease in adults. The pneumococcal bacteria are usually found in the respiratory tract. They can be transferred from one person to another by way of droplets of saliva or mucus, as occurs when the person carrying the organism sneezes, coughs, or kisses someone. It may reach the meninges through the bloodstream, as the result of an ear infection, or in rare cases, by way of a small skull fracture.

Pneumococcal bacteria can be responsible for a wide variety of diseases, including minor ear and sinus infections, pneumonia, and septicemia, in addition to meningitis. Most symptoms of pneumococcal meningitis are the same as for the meningococcal variety.

One type of this bacterum, known as *Streptococcus pneumoniae*, produces exotoxins. Unlike the endotoxins produced by meningococcal bacteria, these poisonous proteins are released by the bacteria while the cells are still alive and whole. Some of these exotoxins are responsible for producing the high fever characteristic of the disease, while others produce a rash on the skin and on the lining of the nose and throat.

Most commonly striking adults, pneumococcal meningitis can be spread by sneezing, coughing, or kissing.

Haemophilus Influenzae **Type b**

Far less common than pneumococcal or meningococcal meningitis is a form of the disease caused by *Haemophilus influenzae* type b, or Hib, which is also found in the nose and throat of most people. The bacterium's name derives from the fact that it appears to thrive on blood (*haemo* in Greek means "blood" and *philus* means "loving"). The second part of the bacterium's name is the result of a misunderstanding. According to the Web site Dr. Greene.com: "When the bacteria were first discovered, they were incorrectly thought to be the cause of influenza. This was disproved a decade before the influenza virus was eventually discovered, but the name for the bacteria had already been in use for a generation, and the name stuck."[11]

Before a vaccine against Hib was developed, this microbe was the leading cause of meningitis in children under five years old.

Neonatal Meningitis

Although young children's chances of developing meningitis have been reduced by vaccines, newborn babies remain at particular risk of meningitis during the first month of life. These cases are caused by various microbes but are classified under the term "neonatal meningitis." The three bacteria responsible for the majority of cases in newborns are *Streptococcus*

A nurse cares for an infant stricken with neonatal meningitis.

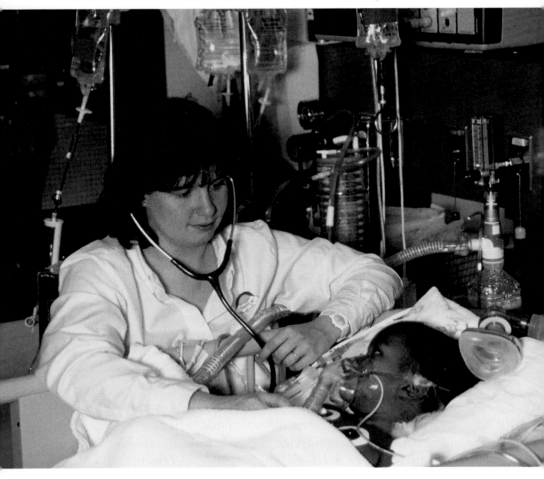

agalactiae (known as group B streptococcus), *Escherichia coli*, and *Listeria monocytogenes*.

Group B streptococcus, or GBS, is the most common agent of neonatal meningitis (70 percent of all cases). It is usually found in the lower gastrointestinal tract, and also the genital tract of approximately one in five expectant mothers. The bacteria is usually harmless and only becomes dangerous when the baby is exposed to it as it passes through the mother's birth canal. Cases of the disease are categorized as early onset (apparent at birth or during the first few days after birth) and late onset (occurring up to two months after birth). In addition to meningitis, GBS infection can also cause septicemia and pneumonia. Although the majority of the approximately 88 percent of babies who survive infection by GBS do not show any severe aftereffects, this is not always the case. Says Estee Torok, a microbiologist at the John Radcliffe Hospital in England, "I have seen some babies who have had GBS meningitis and it can be a devastating disease. In one particular case, a baby was suffering with drowsiness, poor feeding and fits. Unfortunately, the diagnosis of GBS meningitis was delayed and the baby was severely brain damaged."[12]

E. Coli and *Listeria*

Like GBS, most *Escherichia coli*, or *E. coli*, bacteria is harmless, living in the human intestines. It is, in fact, a major component of normal, healthy stool. The variety that causes meningitis in newborns is called K1; as with GBS, exposure occurs during birth, if the baby is exposed to stool. Both GBS- and *E. coli*-caused meningitis can be deadly. The mortality rate in babies infected with *E. coli* is slightly higher (15 percent) than in those infected with GBS (12 percent).

More deadly still is meningitis caused by *Listeria monocytogenes*, which, although it is responsible for only 8 percent of bacterial meningitis cases and is even rarer in neonates, has one of the highest mortality rates (22 percent). It can be contracted from the mother during pregnancy or at birth. It can cross the placental barrier, and infections in late pregnancy may cause a baby to be stillborn. The bacterium is a common food contaminant that can be found almost anywhere, including in soil and dust. Many wild and domesticated animals also carry the bacteria.

Viral Meningitis

Viral meningitis is much more common than bacterial meningitis. Luckily, it is also much less serious, and it often clears on its own within ten days or less. The most common agents of viral meningitis are a group of common viruses known as enteroviruses, more particularly the Coxsackie viruses and echoviruses. Enteroviruses are organisms that attack the digestive system and cause stomach flu. They may be found in the lower intestines and feces. Because of this, they are also found in water and soil polluted by raw sewage. Unlike bacterial meningitis, which is more common in winter, most cases of meningitis caused by enteroviruses occur during the summer months.

Meningitis may also be caused by other viruses, including those that cause influenza, chicken pox, measles, mumps,

Although a rare occurrence, meningitis can be transmitted through the bite of a mosquito.

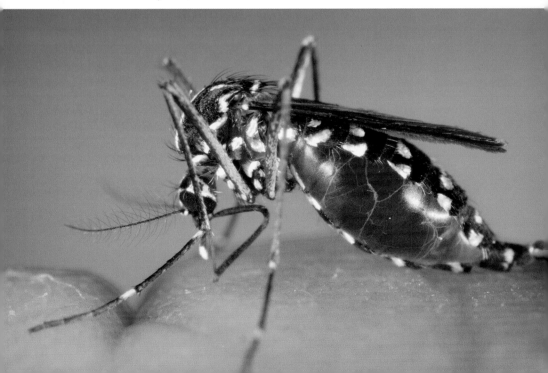

polio, West Nile virus, and herpes sores on the lips and genitals. (The form that used to result as a complication of mumps has been virtually eliminated through the introduction of the measles, mumps, and rubella vaccine.) Although viral meningitis is less serious than the bacterial form of the disease, it can be dangerous when contracted by newborns.

The symptoms of viral meningitis are the same as for the bacterial form of the disease. These include high fever, severe headache, stiff neck, and lethargy. Viral meningitis may occasionally result in a rash that can cover a large portion of the body. This rash, which is red and flat, is different from the one resulting from meningococcal meningitis, which is more localized with tiny, bright red spots covering the body.

Rare Causes

Meningitis can sometimes be caused by organisms usually responsible for other diseases. For example, the bacterium that causes tuberculosis—*Mycobacterium tuberculosis*—can produce meningitis if it invades the meninges by way of the bloodstream. This form of the disease has a very high mortality rate because the onset of symptoms can be very slow; by the time meningitis is suspected, the available treatments are of little use. As many as one in three who contract this form die from the disease, while up to one in four who survive exhibit long-term aftereffects.

Fungi, particularly *Cryptococcus neoformans*, may occasionally cause fungal meningitis. The disease is contracted by inhaling airborne yeast cells. Since the disease can be slow in onset, fungal meningitis is often difficult to diagnose and treat.

Even rarer still are cases of meningitis caused by plasmodium, the parasite that produces malaria. The parasite is transmitted to humans by the bite of a mosquito and is generally limited to countries where malaria is endemic.

Pathogenic and Nonpathogenic Agents

Many of the agents of infection normally reside harmlessly in the nose, throat, or upper respiratory tract of approximately 10 percent of all individuals. Research indicates that this rate may be as high as one in four among young people and college students. This state is called carriage, and the bacteria are called nonpathogenic, or non-disease-producing.

These agents never cause the person to become infected with the disease, since most people have natural resistance to the organisms. The fact that the bacteria cannot live long in the air, and therefore cannot be carried on objects such as clothes, bedding, toys, and furniture, is another reason why the disease is relatively rare.

Upon occasion, however, certain types of bacteria can change the composition of their outer coating into what is called a capsule. The capsule helps the bacteria avoid detection by the body's immune system, allowing the microbe to invade the bloodstream and eventually cause meningitis. The capsule does this by helping the bacteria resemble cells belonging to its host. Says professor Michael Levin of St. Mary's Hospital in London, England:

> The coating of the Group B meningococcus is identical in its structure to the coating of some of the cells within the human brain. And this has been really an extremely clever strategy of the meningococcus. By covering itself in molecules which are identical to molecules within the human body, the immune system is fooled into not recognizing the bacteria. It's almost the Trojan horse sort of strategy."[13]

Once they have acquired this ability to cause illness, the bacteria are called pathogenic. It is estimated that about 10 percent of people are carriers, but only about 1 percent carry pathogenic strains of the disease. Says Dr. Ann Schuchat, acting chief of the Centers for Disease Control and Prevention's respiratory diseases branch, "We continue to try to understand what makes one person get sick and another person just become a carrier."[14]

Scientists hope that if they can unravel that mystery, it will be a significant step in the battle to conquer meningitis. For many patients, it may be the difference between life and death.

CHAPTER TWO

A Medical Emergency

A person suffering from meningitis can become deathly ill within a couple of hours. It is therefore vitally important that he or she receive medical attention as soon as possible. The biggest problem with meningitis is that many of the signs and symptoms displayed by those who have contracted the disease are also associated with several respiratory ailments, including the common cold or flu. As a result, even experienced doctors can fail to realize the grave danger a patient is in. Says Dr. Mark Gardner, director of student health services at Northwestern University: "The initial symptoms mimic influenza, and early cases can pass in and out of emergency rooms and health centers with a diagnosis of flu or bronchitis. Problems occur when people just go home and go to bed and don't notify a doctor when their symptoms change."[15]

Before treatment can begin, a diagnosis must be made. It is vital that the disease be diagnosed as quickly as possible. Says Dr. Matthew Thompson of Oxford University in England, "Since infection can progress from initial symptoms to death within hours, individuals must be diagnosed as early as possible."[16] The diagnosis is based on a variety of factors, including the symptoms exhibited, the patient's medical history, and a physical examination. The doctor usually orders several diagnostic tests to confirm the presence of infection and inflammation. These tests may include a neurological evaluation, a throat culture, any of several imaging techniques, and a spinal tap (lumbar puncture).

Signs and Symptoms

Often, however, valuable time is lost because the patient has no idea how sick he or she is. Meningitis usually begins with flu-like symptoms such as sore throat, nasal congestion, and sometimes muscle aches that develop over the first day or so. Helen, an athletic young college student, remembers feeling tired and having a sore throat. After attending rowing practice, her muscles and joints began aching. "At first," said Helen, "I thought I had overdone the rowing training, but it soon developed into what I thought was the beginning of flu. As the night went on I began to get much worse. I was finding it difficult to stand, I was shivering, shaking and had a severe headache."[17]

The disease's distinguishing characteristics are sudden fever, severe headache, and a stiff neck. Other symptoms might include pain associated with eye movement, an inability to tolerate bright light (photophobia), an inability to straighten the knees in front of the body (Kernig's sign), and severe neck stiffness that causes a patient's hips and knees to flex when the neck is flexed (Brudzinski's sign). Remembered Anne, a mother describing her infant daughter's condition, "Darolyne . . . kept on drawing her legs up to her tummy and her eyes were rolling. She wasn't able to focus and couldn't stand the light."[18]

Sensitivity to sound, drowsiness, irritability, mental confusion, vomiting, severe shooting pain down the neck and along the spine when the neck is bent forward, convulsions or seizures, and coma may also occur. In some severe cases, paralysis may develop on one side of the body. It is especially important to be on the lookout for any of these symptoms in infants. Warns Anne: "Babies and young children are not able to tell anyone how ill they feel. They rely on parents and carers to know the signs and symptoms of meningitis and septicæmia."[19]

The problem is that the early symptoms of meningitis are extremely subtle. Dr. James G. Zimmerly elaborates further:

> The physical examination may not disclose any "classic" signs of meningitis in early stage disease, and the younger the child, the more nonspecific the clinical signs. On occasion the only sign of early meningitis . . . may be a fever,

Early symptoms of meningitis mimic flu symptoms, including severe headache, fever, and stiff neck.

and in infants even the fever is variable. In fact, the early physical examination may be rather unremarkable. Up to 10% of infants with meningitis may appear clinically well on first examination.[20]

Parents of one such infant related their story:

We realized something was wrong when he was just five weeks old and woke up screaming one Tuesday morning. At first we thought he was just hungry but he began crying uncontrollably. We took him to the doctor as we were getting concerned and were advised to take him home and keep a close eye on him. . . .

Harry didn't get any better and became very lethargic.

The doctor called us back at about 4 P.M. to see how Harry was. Again, he had not got any worse or better.

Within an hour of speaking to the doctor it became apparent that Harry was getting worse very quickly. We . . . called the emergency doctor who came to the house. He noticed that the soft spot on Harry's head was tense and bulging and that his breathing was deteriorating. We rushed him to casualty [the emergency room] where he was diagnosed with meningococcal B.[21]

In the case of meningococcal septicemia, one of the distinguishing signs is a bumpy, splotchy, purplish rash that may appear on various parts of the body. Tragically, those who suspect meningitis sometimes wait for the rash to appear before taking action. By then, the patient may be beyond help. Said Linda, whose twenty-two-year-old son died from the disease, "I called the doctors out twice to see David but they said he didn't have meningitis because he didn't have the rash. I know now that we should never have waited for the rash. It cost my son his life."[22]

The rash is actually little bruises caused by the blood leaking out of the tiny capillaries in the skin (and in the organs and tissues of the body) that are being damaged by the disease. In order to test if a rash is the type characteristic of septicemia, a tumbler test may be performed. In this procedure, a clear drinking glass, or tumbler, is pressed firmly against the rash. If it is an ordinary rash, it will fade, or blanch, so that it cannot be seen through the glass. The spots of a septicemic rash, on the other hand, are nonblanching and will still be visible through the side of the glass. If the individual has a dark complexion, spots may appear on paler areas of the skin, such as the palms of the hands or soles of the feet. The rash can occasionally be seen on the whites of the patient's eyes as well.

Red spots caused by meningococcal septicemia will not fade when pressure is applied by, for example, a glass tumbler.

Another type of rash may sometimes be seen in the early stages of meningococcal septicemia. This rash, called a maculopapular rash, does disappear, or blanch, under pressure. Once in a while, both types of rash may appear.

Newborns, however, often will not display these classic signs of meningitis. Instead, they may show what doctors call paradoxical irritability. In this condition, instead of being comforted when picked up and rocked by the mother, the baby becomes even more irritated and distressed. The infant may sometimes display other symptoms, including diarrhea, jaundice (yellowish coloration of the skin), poor feeding, a high-pitched cry, whimpering, stiffness of the body or neck, and a slight fever or lower-than-normal temperature. Occasionally, a parent may notice a swelling on the top of the baby's head at the soft spot (called the fontanel), where the tissue has not yet changed into bone. This swelling is a sign that the disease is already well advanced, since it is caused by the brain itself being forced through the skull's opening.

Amoebic Meningitis

Amoebic meningitis is a rare disease caused by an amoeba—*Naegleria fowleri*—that is usually found in geothermal pools or in stagnating pools of freshwater. It cannot grow in any water body with more than 2 percent salt, such as seawater. Amoebic meningitis was first discovered in the 1960s at the Adelaide Children's Hospital in Australia. Since then, it has been detected in fifteen countries in Asia, Europe, North America, and South America. The disease cannot be passed from person to person, but it is extremely serious and almost always fatal.

The amoeba that causes meningitis may be contracted through the nose of a person who puts his or her head underwater in a geothermal, or natural hot water, pool. In rare instances, it then travels along the nerves to the brain, where it can cause swelling and death. Most victims have been children who were unaware of the dangers of swimming or playing in unclean water.

A pool of stagnant water provides fun but also risk of contamination by the organism that causes amoebic meningitis.

The Doctor's Tools

When a patient coming to a doctor exhibits symptoms that suggest meningitis, the doctor usually tries to eliminate other possible diagnoses and does so as quickly as possible. A medical history is taken in order to review the individual's activities of the past several days. Contact with ill persons, travel, or exposure to insects or animals may suggest an explanation for certain signs or symptoms.

A thorough physical examination is generally the next step. The doctor will usually do this in an isolation room to prevent others from becoming infected. During the examination, the doctor will look for signs of infection around the head, ears, throat, or on the skin along the spine. Blood pressure, pulse, and temperature are also checked.

The physical examination can tell only part of the story, however. Because meningitis affects certain specific parts of the brain, a complete neurological examination is a vital part of the diagnostic process. This type of examination consists of a series of tests of motor and sensory skills, hearing, speech, vision, nerve function, balance, and coordination. Family members may be asked about changes they have observed in the patient's mood or behavior. Older children and adults may be given cognitive tests to assess mental status. The doctor uses a small light, a reflex hammer, a tuning fork, and blunt-pointed pins to evaluate sensory reactions.

The objective of the tests is to identify any abnormalities in the patient's nervous system. Results the doctor may look for include lethargy, photophobia, and difficulty in moving the neck and legs without discomfort.

Throat Culture

Some organisms such as *Neisseria meningitidis* are carried in the upper part of the throat. Since the bacteria can be found in approximately 10 percent of the general population, its presence is not unusual. However, large amounts of the bacteria *Haemophilus influenzae* or *Streptococcus pneumoniae* would be abnormal. Identifying the bacteria that are present

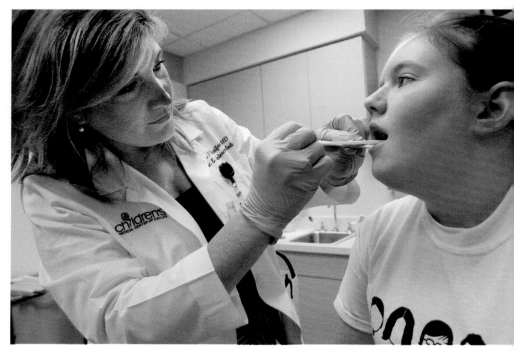

With a simple throat culture (shown), a doctor can test for bacteria such as *Neisseria meningitidis* that live in the throat.

is important in helping the doctor decide on the correct antibiotic for treatment.

To test for these bacteria, the doctor will perform a throat culture. A cotton swab is used to obtain a sample of the material lining the patient's throat. The sample is then placed in a container together with substances that will promote the growth of the organisms in the sample. If disease-causing microbes are found, the culture is said to be positive. In addition to helping determine whether a person has a particular infection, the throat culture can also identify someone who carries a disease and is therefore at risk of transmitting it to others.

Imaging

Modern technology has given doctors additional tools to help them make their diagnoses. Computer-assisted imaging may reveal brain abnormalities such as inflammation or hemorrhaging. Procedures done to diagnose meningitis are computerized tomography (CT scan) and magnetic resonance imaging (MRI). In a CT scan, a computer combines a large number-of X-rays to produce clear three-dimensioned images of the person's internal organs, bones, and tissues. In order to highlight the different tissues, a dye is sometimes injected into the bloodstream. The scan is able to identify conditions such as tumors, cysts, inflammation, blood clots, herniated disks, bone irregularities, and brain damage from head injuries.

An MRI also produces detailed images of body structures, but it uses computer-generated radio waves and a strong magnet

Polymerase Chain Reaction Analysis

A relatively new test used when a doctor suspects meningitis is a polymerase chain reaction (PCR) analysis. The PCR is used to amplify the number of copies of a specific portion of DNA in order to produce enough of the DNA to be tested adequately. It is used to identify disease-causing viruses and does so with a very high degree of accuracy. Dr. John P. Woodall, director of the Nucleus for the Investigation of Emerging Infectious Diseases, Institute for Biomedical Sciences, Federal University of Rio de Janeiro, Brazil, notes that prior to the advent of PCR diagnostic tools,

isolating the [infecting] organism took more than a day, sometimes weeks. Now we've got real-time PCR for more organisms. That has introduced the possibility of getting a diagnosis on the same day, which is important to a treating clinician. In the past, the culture and sensitivity was largely of academic interest because the patient was either dead or discharged before the result came through. Real-time PCR is a tremendous breakthrough.

Quoted in the *Pfizer Journal*, "Staying Ahead in the Germ Wars." www.thepfizer journal.com/default.asp?a=article&j=tpj38&t=Staying%20Ahead%20In%20 The%20Germ%20Wars.

rather than X-rays. In this way, even clearer images can be produced than with a CT scan. The pictures can help pinpoint inflammation in the brain and spinal cord, infection, and blood
vessel irregularities. As with the CT scan, dye is sometimes injected in order to enhance contrast and produce more detailed
images. Using these imaging techniques, physicians can detect
the inflammation that is characteristic of meningitis.

Lumbar Puncture

Although modern imaging techniques can pinpoint the inflammation associated with meningitis, it cannot tell the doctor
what microbe is to blame. Lumbar puncture is a medical procedure in which a small sample of cerebrospinal fluid is removed and examined. Commonly referred to as a spinal tap,
the procedure is generally done in order to test for meningitis.
It is relatively easy to perform, is fairly inexpensive, and best
of all it allows the doctor to know exactly what organism is
causing the problem. Because of this, it is considered the gold
standard for diagnosing meningitis.

In a spinal tap, the individual is positioned so that the spaces
between the vertebrae (the bones of the spine) are as wide as
possible. After the area has been cleaned and the skin numbed
by an injection of a local anesthetic called lidocaine, a small,
hollow needle is inserted, usually between the third and fourth
lumbar vertebrae in the lower back. Although it may be uncom-
fortable, the procedure is usually not very painful.

A few drops of cerebrospinal fluid are drawn and sent to a
lab to be examined. At the lab, the fluid is tested in three ways:
to determine its chemical composition, to examine the cells
floating in it, and to look for evidence that it is infected. Since
the body produces white blood cells in order to fight infection,
their presence in the cerebrospinal fluid is an indication of
meningitis. So, too, is a lower percentage of glucose, since the
bacteria consume the glucose for their own nourishment. An
analysis of the cerebrospinal fluid may also help the doctor to
identify the exact type of bacteria that is causing the meningitis.

As helpful as the spinal tap can be in making the diagnosis,
there are times when a doctor cannot perform one. For exam-

Doctors from the World Health Organization perform lumbar punctures to test spinal fluid for meningitis in Africa.

ple, occasionally the amount of brain swelling may be so great that a lumbar puncture, by releasing pressure in the spine, would cause the brain to be forced into the top of the spinal column. Such an event, known as "coning," can be fatal.

Treatment

Usually, however, the spinal tap can be safely done, and the nature of infection in the cerebrospinal fluid determines which antibiotic is prescribed. In any case, the seriousness of acute bacterial meningitis requires that the antibiotics be administered as soon as possible in order to ensure the greatest probability of recovery and the least risk of complications. Until

Getting Around the Blood-Brain Barrier

The endothelial cells that make up the walls of the capillaries in the brain are joined together very tightly at their edges. Because of this, they prevent most larger molecules carried by the bloodstream from passing through them and moving into the brain. This is known as the blood-brain barrier. The problem is that most of the drugs used to treat brain diseases are made up of such large molecules. Scientists have been working for years to find a way around this problem.

One method involves adding excess sugar to the bloodstream. Before the sugar can be cleaned up by the body's insulin system, it extracts water from the endothelial cells, making them shrivel. The tight junctions between these cells in the brain open up for a brief period of time so that a greater amount of the drug can pass through the blood-brain barrier. A second, more promising method involves latching chemical agents onto molecules that already have brain access.

Although each of these methods has its disadvantages, they are both preferable to the one used by William Pardridge in a 2001 experiment with rats. Pardridge bypassed the blood-brain barrier by simply drilling a hole in a rat's skull and injecting a drug directly into the animal's brain.

around the 1980s, penicillin was the preferred drug. Unfortunately, many bacteria developed resistance to it, and other antibiotics had to be used.

Depending on the bacterial strain encountered, the doctor will order treatment with ampicillin, cefotaxime, cephalosporin, chloramphenicol, deftriaxone, or gentamicin. Naturally, the patient must be closely watched. Some people are allergic to particular antibiotics, and a reaction can be life threatening. In addition, some drugs may occasionally cause problems such as liver or kidney damage, in which case a different antibiotic will be required.

One difficulty with treating meningitis is that many of the most effective drugs cannot cross the blood-brain barrier. To start working, therefore, they must be injected directly into the cerebrospinal fluid. Such procedures are done by means of lumbar puncture.

In the case of viral meningitis, antibiotics are generally useless. (One exception is the type caused by the herpes virus, which can be treated with acyclovir.) Fortunately, the viral form of the illness goes away on its own. Depending on the severity of the infection, sufferers may be hospitalized or treated at home. The normal course of treatment includes bed rest, lots of fluids, and analgesics such as aspirin or ibuprofen for relief of pain and fever.

One thing patients may do to help them fight off the effects of the virus is to avoid foods with a high sugar content. Explains Dr. Nancy Appleton, "The bottom line is that sugar upsets the body chemistry and suppresses the immune system. Once the immune system becomes suppressed, the door is opened to infectious and degenerative diseases. The stronger the immune system the easier it is for the body to fight infections and degenerative diseases."[23]

Inflammation of the meninges is generally less severe in viral meningitis than in bacterial meningitis, and the body is usually able to repair any injury to the tissue. In cases where inflammation is more severe, steroids may be prescribed along with sedatives and pain medication to ease the patient's discomfort. Anticonvulsants may also be prescribed to prevent seizures.

In the case of fungal meningitis, amphotericin B, administered intravenously, is the most common treatment. If a patient fails to respond to this, medication may be dispensed directly into the spinal fluid (intrathecal medication). On occasion, the oral medication fluconazone may also be used.

Steroids

Since the late 1980s, data from some clinical trials have shown that early therapy with steroids can be beneficial in the treatment of bacterial meningitis in children. According to an article in *Current Treatment Options in Infectious Diseases*, dexamethasone (a steroid) is recommended by the American Academy of Pediatrics. Dr. Carina A. Rodriguez and Dr. Elaine I. Tuomanen report, "The clearest beneficial impact was demonstrated for *Haemophilus* infection. Supportive evidence in the case of pneumococcal disease has been obtained, but the studies are less conclusive. No trials have been done in adults, leaving the decision to use steroids in this age group at the discretion of the attending physician."[24]

A patient receives medication intravenously, a method commonly used to treat fungal meningitis.

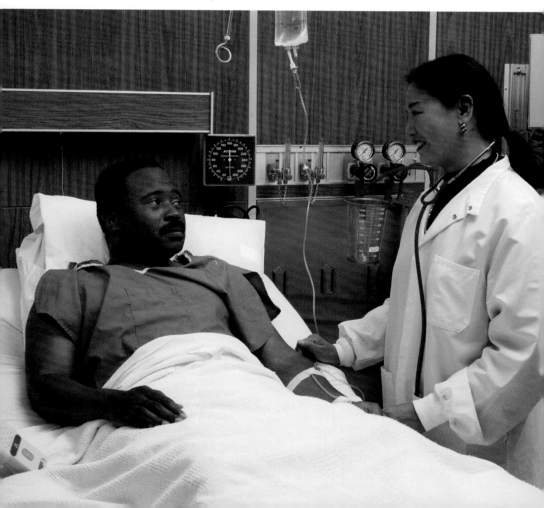

This approach has not generally been used on adult patients. Still, some evidence suggests that steroids may help reduce deaths and neurological damage from bacterial meningitis. Many doctors disagree, saying that the relatively small number of test cases provides too little support for using steroids.

Those who favor including steroids in the treatment of meningitis note that effectiveness may depend on what form of the disease a patient has. In a 2002 study, researchers found that when a steroid was administered together with antibiotics, the risk of death was reduced by as much as half in instances where the patient had contracted the pneumococcus bacteria. The study also reported fewer individuals suffering serious complications. Hearing loss in children treated with antibiotics and dexamethasone was also reduced. Results were not conclusive, however, when a combination of antibiotics and steroids were administered to patients suffering with meningococcal meningitis.

Scientists continue to look at steroids as a possible addition to the standard treatments, however. The deadliness of meningitis and its rapid onset are reasons enough to explore any and all leads in the search for answers.

CHAPTER THREE

Preventing Meningitis

The serious nature of meningitis and the uncertainty of success in treating it means that the best approach is avoiding the disease altogether. There are several vaccines that can be used against various bacteria that cause meningitis. Just as important are the commonsense steps individuals can take to make themselves less susceptible to the disease.

Those Most at Risk

Preventing meningitis is everyone's concern, since the disease can strike at any age. The groups most at risk, however, are children under two, young adults aged fourteen to twenty-five, and adults aged fifty-five and over. For reasons that are unclear, males suffer from meningitis at a higher rate than females. Because meningitis is a communicable disease, those who come in close contact with someone who has the disease are also at risk. An individual living in an infected household may have as much as eight hundred times the risk of catching meningitis as a person living elsewhere. Moreover, this increased risk can last for as long as a month after the victim has been diagnosed and treated.

The incidence of meningitis is higher in nonindustrialized regions of the world. These regions include sub-Saharan Africa and parts of Asia and South America. In addition to the local populace, persons traveling to those areas are at higher risk. The risk naturally increases in direct proportion to the length of the stay and the level of contact with local populations. In 2000 and 2001, an international outbreak of meningococcal infection was associated with the hajj, the Islamic pilgrimage to Mecca in Saudi Arabia. Over three hundred pilgrims were infected with *Neisseria meningitidis* W135. These travelers, in turn, brought it back to their home countries upon their return. Worldwide, seventy-one deaths were attributed to the outbreak. Iain Simpson, spokesman for the World Health Organization, noted that the crowded sleeping conditions among the pilgrims made the spread of the disease particularly easy. The strain of the disease that struck the pilgrims, which had not appeared in the region prior to 2000, was also responsible for an epidemic that struck thirteen thousand people and claimed more than fifteen hundred lives in the African nation of Burkina Faso two years later. Because of the outbreaks, a certificate of vaccination against meningococcal meningitis is now an entry requirement for all pilgrims on the hajj.

Outbreaks of meningococcal infection linked to Islamic pilgrims in Mecca forced residents and visitors to don masks.

College Students at Risk

As the outbreak among the pilgrims to Mecca suggests, meningitis thrives where people live in close quarters. This may explain why college students living in dormitories are at increased risk. Beyond the close living conditions of a dorm, there are likely other factors at work on college campuses. The bacteria that cause the disease must pass through the mucosa, a moist layer of tissue that lines the respiratory tract, in order to cause an infection. Researchers say that smoking or living in a smoky environment damages this mucosa, and such conditions are not uncommon on many college campuses. Data also suggest that behaviors such as excessive alcohol consumption, visiting bars, and sleeping irregularly—again, common among college students—increase risk. Stress is also considered a possible contributing factor. Since stress is often a part of the daily life of college freshmen, who are entering a new phase of life, some scientists think this might explain why this particular group is six times as likely as other college students to contract meningitis.

Prior to 1971 the military had seen a higher incidence of meningitis than the overall population. Indeed, meningitis was often referred to as "a disease of children and soldiers" because of its tendency to affect these two groups at a higher rate than the general population. As is the case with college students, military recruits live in close contact with each other in confined areas. Outbreaks of meningococcal group C disease in U.S. Army boot camps in the 1960s spurred research aimed at developing an effective vaccine. Routine vaccination of recruits was implemented. The result was an 87 percent reduction in sporadic cases of the disease and the virtual elimination of outbreaks—that is, two or more cases—of meningococcal meningitis in the American military.

Not surprisingly, individuals with weakened immune systems are also more susceptible to meningitis than the population at large. This includes those with AIDS. Others who seem to be at high risk are people who have had their spleen removed or damaged. This is because the spleen plays a key role in the functioning of the body's immune system.

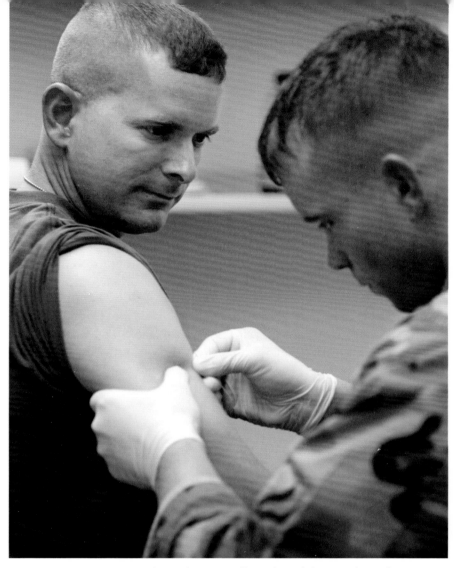

Routine vaccinations have dramatically reduced the number of meningococcal cases in the American military.

Other medical factors that increase the risk of various forms of meningitis include poor overall health; low birth weight; having a birth defect involving formation of the skull; a history of pulmonary tuberculosis; undergoing procedures in which foreign objects are surgically placed in the skull (such as tubes to drain abnormal amounts of accumulated cerebrospinal fluid); undergoing treatment with a kidney dialysis machine; undergoing drug therapy that suppresses the immune system, such as that following organ transplantation or treatment for cancer;

contracting certain other infections such as mumps, tuberculosis, syphilis, and Lyme disease; undergoing a cochlear implant for severe hearing loss; and having had meningitis in the past.

Certain genetic factors have been recognized by scientists as adversely affecting a body's ability to mount an effective defense against the meningitis bacteria. One of these is a condition known as complement component deficiency. Explains Dr. Rodrigo Hasbun, an associate professor of medicine at Tulane University School of Medicine, "The first thing that has been well-known for several years is complement deficiency. Patients that have genetically deficient complement are definitely at higher risk of having the disease."[25] Complements are enzymes in the blood serum that join forces with antibodies to kill various types of bacteria. If they are lacking, antibodies cannot do their job efficiently. Similarly, mannose-binding lectin is a protein that helps the complement bind to the antibody. If it is defective or missing, the body's immune system cannot work properly.

Susceptibility by Age

Newborns who contract meningitis usually do so through their mothers. Nowadays, the most common agent in those babies up to the age of three months is the group B *streptococcus*, which often grows in the female genital tract. *E. coli* and *Listeria monocytogenes* also account for a significant number of cases.

From age three months to eighteen years, *Neisseria meningitidis* is the most common bacterial cause of infection. This agent is the only one responsible for causing epidemics of meningitis. Outbreaks have been known to occur where an infected individual has been exposed to others in a crowded environment, such as a child in a day-care center, a college student in a dormitory, or a military recruit in a training camp. In addition to *Neisseria meningitidis*, individuals in this age bracket are also especially susceptible to *Streptococcus pneumoniae* and *Haemophilus influenzae*.

Among adults over eighteen years of age, a common cause of bacterial meningitis is *Streptococcus pneumoniae*. For many years, *Haemophilus influenzae* type b, or Hib, was the leading cause of bacterial meningitis among children under five years of age in the United States. Since the introduction of the immunization of children for Hib in the late 1980s, the number of cases of this type of meningitis in youngsters has decreased drastically. Over a period of ten years (1986 to 1995), the median age of patients suffering from Hib-caused meningitis rose from fifteen months to twenty-five years. In the industrialized world, Hib meningitis has a low death rate of approximately 5 percent. Around 12 percent of those who survive may suffer permanent aftereffects.

Over the same time period, the rate for *Neisseria meningitidis* has remained relatively constant at 14 to 25 percent. *Streptococcus pneumoniae* has taken over as the most common cause of meningitis overall, accounting for 47 percent of all cases. At 19 to 26 percent, it also has one of the highest mortality rates among bacterial agents causing meningitis.

Prevention

No matter who is at risk or why, the serious nature of the disease means that preventing infection in the first place is a vital concern. Meningitis and meningococcal septicemia can be prevented by building up immunity to the bacteria, either naturally or by vaccination. Steps taken to do this are dependent on the risk groups involved.

Newborns, for example, rarely get the types of meningitis caused by *Neisseria meningitidis, Streptococcus pneumoniae*, or Hib simply because they rarely come in contact with these germs in the first few days of life. In addition, newborn babies retain a temporary immunity that comes from the mother's immune system.

The agents more likely to bring on the disease in newborns are *E. coli* and group B streptococcus, both of which may be present in the mother's genital tract. Since women displaying large amounts of either of these agents are known to have a higher chance of giving birth to a baby who later develops meningitis, the best method of prevention is to ensure that they receive treatments prior to giving birth.

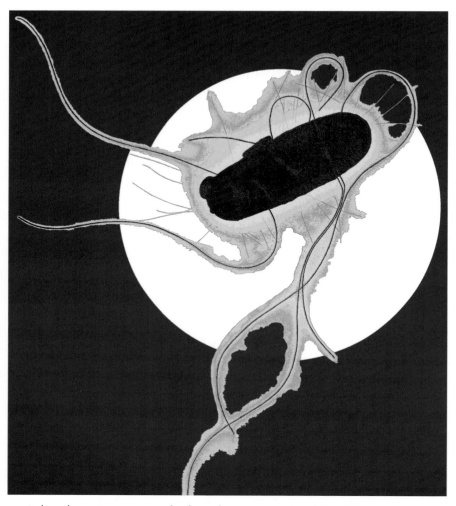

Babies born to women who have large amounts of *E. coli* in their system are at risk for developing meningitis. An *E. coli* bacterium is pictured here in a colored micrograph.

For just about anyone, however, preventing exposure to infectious agents is extremely important. Care should be taken to avoid sharing anything that may have touched the mouth of an infected person. Hands should be washed thoroughly with soap and water, particularly after coming in contact with surfaces in public bathrooms or other crowded areas where microbes can breed. Of course, any actions that help the immune system to function better will help ward off infection. Getting adequate rest, eating a well-balanced diet with lots of fresh fruits and vegetables, exercising regularly, and avoiding excessive stress all do their part to strengthen the body's immune system.

Chemoprophylaxis

Experts say that in addition to the body's natural defenses, chemoprophylaxis (the administration of a medication for the purpose of preventing a disease) is also a useful tool in the battle against meningitis. Antibiotics, for example, are usually administered to those people living in the same household as the

Alternative Therapies

Alternative therapies such as nutritional and herbal therapies are sometimes used in conjunction with conventional treatment of meningitis, but not in place of it. Some studies suggest that herbal therapies under the supervision of a health professional may help fight microbes and help regulate the immune system in the treatment of certain types of meningitis. One study, for example, has suggested that patients with tuberculous meningitis have decreased levels of vitamin B_{12} while another found that a vitamin A deficiency may play a role in meningococcal disease in the meningitis belt. In laboratory tests, garlic has been shown to have an effect in slowing the growth of the fungus *Cryptococcus neoformans*, while echinacea has significantly improved the immune function in animals. Further research needs to be done to determine whether these substances can help treat meningitis in humans.

Practitioners of homeopathic medicine believe that some symptoms can be relieved by administering minute doses of substances that normally are toxic in larger quantities. Homeopathic remedies are made from naturally occurring plant, animal, or mineral substances. Again, such treatments should only be conducted under the supervision of a trained and certified homeopathic doctor.

patient and to his or her close contacts. Casual contacts and even hospital personnel treating patients do not appear to be at increased risk of getting the disease. The exceptions would be those who perform mouth-to-mouth resuscitation on a patient. According to research published in the *British Medical Journal*, such individuals are six and a half times more likely to catch the disease than less intimate contacts and almost eighteen times as likely as the population at large.

The antibiotic of choice for those exposed to some form of bacterial meningitis is rifampin, with ciprofloxacin also occasionally used. Experts caution, though, that these drugs are mostly useful in preventing the disease from spreading to others by stopping the growth of any meningococcal bacteria that might be lurking in the nose or throat. These antibiotics will not be effective against bacteria that have already invaded the body. As a result, a person who has been exposed should still be watchful for symptoms of the disease.

Chemoprophylaxis is somewhat controversial, however. The *British Medical Journal* maintains that chemoprophylaxis "may be prescribed in excess of what is needed."[26] The danger in the use of antibiotics to prevent illness is that it may lead to the development of strains of the disease-causing bacteria that are resistant to antibiotics. Such was the case in Norway, where in 1970 a strain of resistant microbes was found. Since then, chemoprophylaxis for the disease has been banned in that country.

Vaccination

Many experts believe that the greatest promise for prevention of meningitis lies in vaccination. In industrialized nations, vaccination programs have dramatically reduced the incidence of Hib-caused meningitis, particularly in children. The Hib vaccine also reduces carriage of the bacteria, since the immune response knocks out the small number of bacteria harbored by a carrier. This effect is known as herd immunity.

In addition to the success of the Hib vaccine, other vaccines are available that can protect adults against many forms of *Neisseria meningitidis*. No vaccine currently available in the

United States, however, can protect against serogroup B meningitis. This is because the bacteria of this strain carry chemical tags on their surface that are very similar to those found in certain human cells. Because the immune system fails to recognize these organisms as foreign, vaccines based on these cells would produce only a very weak response, if any at all. In addition, vaccines have not yet been proven effective against *Streptococcus pneumoniae* or forms of the disease caused by fungal, amoebic, or viral agents.

Concerned family members watch a tearful youngster receive a meningitis vaccine in China.

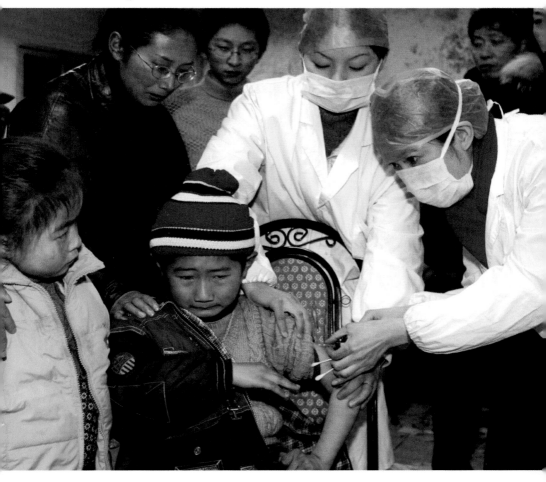

Although vaccines can prevent certain forms of meningitis, some experts say that universal vaccination is not the answer. For one thing, underdeveloped countries are often unable to afford to implement vaccination programs on a scale large enough to be effective. Sometimes, prevention seems not to be worth the expense, even in developed countries. Explains Dr. James Turner of the University of Virginia:

> When governments and health agencies recommend universal vaccination, they've done an analysis that demonstrates that the cost of vaccinating the population is less than the cost of the disease burden to society. When you apply that analysis to meningococcal disease, because it is so rare, it is not cost effective to society to vaccinate all of these individuals.[27]

According to figures from the Centers for Disease Control and Prevention, vaccinating all college freshmen, for example, would cost approximately 130 million dollars. Since this would prevent just forty to seventy cases of meningitis and save only two to four lives each year, it is not considered by those in charge of public health policy worth the tax dollars involved. Such calculations, naturally, cannot factor in the suffering the disease imposes on those few victims and their families.

College Immunizations

The answer to this cost-versus-benefit dilemma seems to be the easy availability of vaccination for those who want it. The Advisory Committee on Immunization Practices and the American College Health Association states, when it comes to preventing meningitis on campus, "vaccination should be provided or made easily available to those freshmen who wish to reduce their risk of disease. Other undergraduate students wishing to reduce their risk of meningococcal disease can also choose to be vaccinated."[28] Turner who is also chairman of the Preventable Disease Task Force at the American College Health Association agrees, saying, "It can be lifesaving for an individual or a family and is about the same cost as a cheap algebra book."[29] As of July 2005, thirty-three states had passed legislation requir-

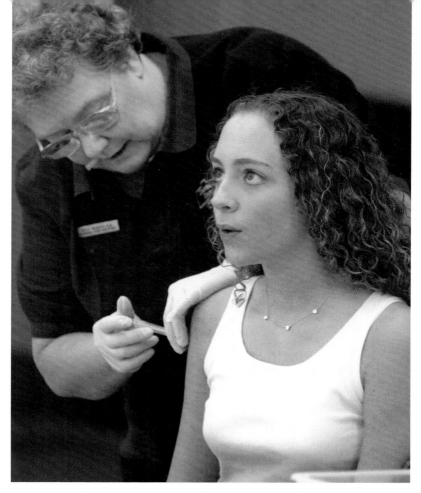

A number of states have enacted laws requiring colleges to vaccinate students like this young woman against meningitis.

ing colleges either to educate students and parents about meningococcal meningitis vaccination or mandate vaccination unless parents sign a waiver.

Although most vaccines are safe to use, individuals may occasionally show mild reactions to them. The most common reactions are redness or swelling around the site of the injection, slight fever, and headaches. Rarer reactions include dizziness, swollen glands, and a rash. These side effects generally disappear within a short period of time. Experts note that these mild reactions are a small price to pay for protection against a disease that can kill in a matter of hours or that can leave a survivor disabled for life.

CHAPTER FOUR

A Lifetime of Consequences

John was a robust, 6-foot-4-inch (193cm), 210-pound (95km) basketball player at a New England college. One night, the nineteen-year-old freshman came down with a high fever and other flu-like symptoms. By the next morning, he was in a hospital emergency room fighting for his life. He was soon diagnosed with meningococcal meningitis. Despite receiving massive doses of antibiotics, John's body was quickly ravaged by the disease. One emergency room doctor said it was like watching a house burn down.

As his family gathered around John, a priest administered last rites. Miraculously, however, John clung to life. Unfortunately, the disease had wreaked havoc on his body. Said his mother, "He was bleeding from the nose, ears and eyes, and his fingers started dying."[30] John survived, but gangrene, the death or decay of the tissue in a part of the body, had set in. Doctors were forced to amputate his right leg below the knee, all of his fingers, and the toes on his left foot.

A Long Battle

As John's experience demonstrates, the battle to overcome meningitis or meningococcal septicemia does not necessarily end when the patient leaves the hospital. Although some patients make a fast, complete recovery, many others require

58

support and care for a long time afterward. The aftereffects that afflict them may be permanent, causing physical disabilities or the far less obvious psychological ones. Others will improve and eventually disappear over time.

John is one of many who continue to deal with the effects of meningitis even after the disease has been purged from their bodies. Although these aftereffects and complications can happen with any form of the disease, they are much more common among victims of meningococcal meningitis. Still, those who have had pneumococcal meningitis are also frequently left disabled. Those who contracted the disease as newborns are also at high risk of suffering long-term disabilities.

The exact numbers are not known, but the Meningitis Trust estimates that "15% of sufferers are left with serious disabilities and many more will suffer a range of short-term or less

Some meningitis victims like Scottish lawyer Olivia Giles (right), require the amputation of limbs, due to gangrenous infections.

serious problems."[31] Some experts see this figure as low, instead saying that short-term effects occur in one out of four people who survive meningitis or septicemia. Many of those who suffer from viral meningitis exhibit similar aftereffects, but rarely are these as severe as the ones associated with bacterial forms of the disease.

According to the Meningitis Trust, the most commonly reported aftereffects found in both children and adults include general fatigue, headaches, difficulty in concentrating, short-term memory loss, lack of coordination, balance problems, de-

The Meningitis Trust

The Meningitis Trust is an international charity established in the United Kingdom in 1986 by a group of parents directly affected by the meningitis outbreak in the Stroud-Stonehouse area of Gloucestershire in the mid-1980s. Explains founder Jane Wells on the Meningitis Trust's Web site:

> When my son had meningitis during the outbreak in Stroud in 1986 I was devastated, and desperate to talk to someone who knew how I felt. But there simply wasn't the information and support available. The outbreak soon hit the headlines and I found myself taking calls from parents all over the UK. That was the beginnings of our first Helpline and the Meningitis Trust.

The mission of the Meningitis Trust is "continuing to be the world authority on meningitis, leading the fight against the disease and empowering people and organizations through collaborative working, to reduce the threat of meningitis and its impact on people everywhere." It attempts to raise awareness about the disease, provides counseling services, and offers a range of educational programs tailored for health professionals. The Meningitis Trust also funds research into all aspects of the disease.

Quoted in Meningitis Trust, "About Us." www.meningitis-trust.org/about_us.

pression, violent temper tantrums, bouts of aggression, mood swings, learning difficulties, scarring and loss of digits or limbs (in cases of septicemia), hearing impairment or deafness, tinnitus (ringing in the ears), sore or stiff joints, eyesight problems, kidney and adrenal gland failure, epilepsy, and brain damage. Thirty-year-old Sandra's problems are not unusual. "I have bladder and bowel problems," she explains, "and walk with crutches. My balance is not so good some days because of the spastic muscles and the weakness in my legs and my left arm. Sometimes it takes all my strength just to do the little things."[32]

Young children may also exhibit babyish behavior such as being extra clingy, throwing temper tantrums, forgetting recently learned skills, demanding attention, bed-wetting, waking up during the night with nightmares, and sleepwalking.

When infants are involved, aftereffects may not make themselves known until some time later. Relates one parent:

> My son had pneumococcal meningitis when he was six months old. He has always been difficult but it wasn't until he started school that it was discovered he had behavioral and social difficulties, and was also hyperactive. He is now on medication and it has finally been confirmed that the meningitis caused his difficulties. He has been assessed for special needs and is trying out a new school, having been excluded from the first one."[33]

Physical Aftereffects

In addition to behavioral difficulties, meningitis patients suffer from physical aftereffects that are usually determined by the part of the brain affected. In many cases, the nerves responsible for hearing are damaged, resulting in problems ranging from mild hearing loss to total deafness in one or both ears. Indeed, some degree of hearing loss is the most common aftereffect of meningitis. Reported one meningitis survivor:

> Having meningococcal meningitis 15 years ago at the age of 15 left me totally deafened. This completely changed my life and lives of my family and friends. The problems associated with being deaf are many: learning to lip-read, relying

New York writer Ved Mehta (pictured in 1984) lost his sight to meningitis as a young boy.

on others for telephone communication and limited employment prospects are among them. However, after many trials and tribulations I am now living as full a life as possible and have recently had a cochlear implant which has greatly improved my quality of life. There is hope after meningitis—even if left with a severe disability.[34]

Those who have survived a bout with meningitis also sometimes suffer from some loss of eyesight. Experts say this may be due to pressure the swollen brain tissue exerts on the optic nerve. The blindness may be in either one or both eyes. Depending on the culture the patient comes from, the consequences of blindness (or other disabilities) extend far beyond the physical impediments. Such was the case with Ved Mehta, a staff writer for the *New Yorker* magazine for thirty-three years, who lost his sight to meningitis before his fourth birthday. Writes Mehta: "Hindus consider blindness a punishment for sins committed in a previous incarnation. But my father, a doctor, tried to fight the superstition and give me an education, like his other children, so that I could become . . . a self-supporting citizen of the world."[35]

Fortunately for those who suffer post-meningitis sight loss, the blindness commonly is temporary. This aftereffect usually disappears over time, and eyesight returns to normal.

Amputations

Problems resulting from meningitis that affect hearing and sight may be temporary. Other aftereffects from the disease may be more permanent. The aftereffects of septicemia may result in major damage to body organs. Permanent scarring may be one outcome. More serious damage may require skin grafts or plastic surgery to correct.

In those patients for whom the damage is so severe as to require amputation of toes, fingers, legs, or arms, the shock alone can be a major challenge. When John awoke from the coma induced by his illness, he was devastated to find that his right leg and all of his fingers had been amputated. "I freaked out when I found out what I'd lost," he remembered. "Sometimes I'd ask, 'Why me?' Then I'd see other people at the rehab hospital who were worse than I was."[36]

After recovering from his disease, John traveled around to area high schools to warn other young people about the dangers of meningitis. As part of his talk, he would demonstrate what it was like to suffer his losses. "I'd wrap up one of the students' hands in an Ace bandage," said John, "then throw him a bag of candy and tell him to open it and pass the candies around. When the kids saw how hard it was to do without fingers, it opened their eyes to what this disease is all about."[37]

Seventeen-year-old Nick had a similar experience upon awakening from the coma caused by his disease. "As I opened my eyes," he recalled, "I saw my dad sitting by my bed. 'I don't think I have fingers anymore,' I whispered to him. He sat there silent, but shaking, for about a minute—and I could tell he was fighting back tears. 'Nick,' he finally said, 'they had to cut your fingers off.'"[38]

Nick, like John, has fought back from his illness. He volunteers with the National Meningitis Association and tries to

The Duchess of Cornwall, wife of Britain's Prince Charles, laughs with a young meningitis amputee. The courageous girl participates in sports and dance.

make teens aware of the benefits of getting vaccinated against the disease that has altered his life so drastically.

Amputees such as John and Nick may be fitted for prosthetic limbs, but these devices often present their own set of concerns, including skin problems. Says Nick, "It took me months to learn to walk again because my first pair of prosthetic legs rubbed the skin on my stumps right off, which was so painful."[39]

Persons who are candidates for a prosthesis will require several visits to a facility to be fitted correctly. Physical or occupational therapy may be needed in order to assist the individual in helping him or her regain independence. Professional assistance may also be required to help some survivors make the emotional adjustment to the loss of a limb.

Living as an Amputee

Despite facing such adversity, with determination and the support of their families, many of these meningitis survivors are able to lead normal lives for the most part. Seven-year-old Thomas had to endure the amputation of his left hand, the toes on his left foot, the fingertips of his right hand, and two toes of his right foot. Despite this, he has learned to walk again and now rides his bike, plays football, participates in judo, and swims. How readily a patient adjusts depends on attitude. Remembers Thomas's mother, "He wanted to go back to school the day after he came out of the ward."[40]

Since the loss of a limb may result in decreased activity, it can also lead to an increased risk of the kind of health problems associated with a sedentary lifestyle. Such problems are not limited to the obvious, such as a loss of physical strength and poor muscle tone. The results of one recent study attributed 20 percent of all deaths of people thirty-five and older to a lack of physical activity. The study reported that the risk of dying from cancer increased 45 percent for men and 28 percent for women, the risk of dying from heart disease was 52 percent higher for men and 28 percent higher for women, and the risk of dying from respiratory ailments was 92 percent higher for men and 75 percent higher for women. Clearly, then, meningitis survivors face a host of potential challenges.

Other complications faced by survivors may include seizures, the result of damage caused by the brain's swelling. Although seizures are a rather rare aftereffect, those who suffer from them may require long-term medication.

Short-term memory loss and difficulty concentrating are more common aftereffects of meningitis. These may make even the simplest of everyday chores a challenge. Nineteen-year-old Carolyn experienced memory loss and some damage to her speech center. Once her doctor asked her how old she was and she replied, "Fourteen." Later, she explained, "I'd mean to say one thing but say something else, even though I knew I was saying it wrong."[41] Carolyn's speech eventually improved, but her memory had either been destroyed or was seriously impaired. She had to learn all over again, beginning at the first-grade level. She first learned the alphabet, then how to count. Her perseverance was rewarded, and within half a year she had successfully sailed through eight grades of learning.

Psychological and Emotional Aftereffects

Some doctors who treat meningitis patients believe its psychological and emotional aftereffects are harder to quantify, since it is sometimes difficult to know if an effect is a direct result of the disease or the product of the trauma associated with a stay in the hospital. Some people who are seriously ill with meningitis may spend weeks in intensive care. Such confinement in itself can often be an unsettling experience for both the patient and his or her family.

Moreover, some patients report that their emotional state changes from day to day. The age of the patient also plays a role. Adult survivors report experiencing periods of depression and anxiety, while teenagers and older children may demonstrate a lack of self-esteem and confidence, together with mood swings.

Some people try to return to work as soon as possible to show that they have returned to full health. This can sometimes be a mistake since the recuperating body may not yet be adequately able to handle the stress that is a regular part of a daily work routine. Says twenty-six-year-old Cassie: "Returning to work too soon has hampered my recovery. I experience

Steve Elkington

Steve Elkington has been a professional golfer since 1985. He has won ten tournaments on the Professional Golfers Association (PGA) Tour, including the 1995 PGA Championship. In his golfing career, Elkington has had to overcome numerous health problems, including grass allergies, a malignant growth on his shoulder, and sinus problems that required surgery. He has also had viral meningitis four times.

The medical community has been unable to tell him the reason for his recurrent disease. As he told *Golf Digest* in a 1999 interview, "The doctors say it has nothing to do with my allergies, 'necessarily.' It has nothing to do with my antibiotics, 'necessarily.' Nothing to do with my immune system, 'necessarily.' Nothing to do with stress, 'necessarily.'"

Elkington believes his bouts with the disease are related to his allergy problems. Unfortunately, as a pro golfer, it's hard for him to avoid coming in contact with grass. His bouts with meningitis begin with a headache that builds and builds until it feels like "a forest fire in your head." Still, Elkington refuses to let his ailment stop him from becoming one of the top golfers in the world. As he puts it, "There's no reason to think my swing's gone or my game's gone because of a headache."

Quoted in *Golf Digest*, "Elkington's Recurring Malady—Golfer Steve Elkington and Meningitis," August 1999.

Steve Elkington celebrates his 1995 PGA win with his wife and daughter.

panic attacks, extreme tiredness, and often become short-tempered, which is completely out of character."[42]

Experts note that the less stress a patient has when recuperating, the faster his or her condition will improve. Stress causes the body to raise blood pressure and lower the effectiveness of the immune system. If left uncontrolled, stress also can lead to depression, fatigue, tension headaches, migraines, ulcers, and a variety of other disorders. In this regard, complementary treatments such as acupuncture, aromatherapy, hypnotherapy, and homeopathy may be helpful to some sufferers in their struggle with aftereffects.

Bereavement

The consequences of meningitis extend far beyond those who are stricken. This is particularly true for the families of those who succumb to the disease. The loss of a loved one is one of life's most stressful events. It gives way to a feeling of bereavement, which literally means "to be deprived by death." This event can be even more stressful when the death is sudden and unexpected. One of the most upsetting aspects of losing someone to meningitis is the speed with which the disease develops and runs its course. A person may die within hours of first contracting the disease.

The bereaved experiences a range of emotions, which may include anger, confusion, denial, despair, disbelief, guilt, humiliation, numbness, resentment, sadness, shock, and yearning. These feelings are normal and appropriate in a person faced with such a loss and may remain with an individual for weeks, months, or even years. Over time, the intensity of these painful feelings diminishes although for most the pain never goes away completely. Those who have suffered such loss say it is vital that those left behind have as much support as possible from other family members in order to cope successfully with these emotions.

The Support of Family and Friends

Even when the meningitis victim survives, complete recovery, both physical and emotional, may take months or even years. The help and support of an individual's family and friends is

A young mother mourns the sudden death of her nine-month-old daughter from meningitis.

most important during this time. Says Nola, who was stricken with a rare form of meningitis at the age of forty-three:

> Although I have regained the use of my legs, I have had to cope with the loss of my hearing (attributed to one of the drugs used to treat the meningitis), as well as ongoing problems with balance, headaches, incontinence and fatigue. The meningitis destroyed a part of my life which I will never get back. I believe I am lucky to be alive and for that I have to thank my family and the doctors, all of whom worked so hard to make me well.[43]

Some other survivors are not as lucky. Relates Gaynor, "I grew up in the late fifties-early sixties when not as much was known about meningitis then as now. My mother didn't recognize the effects of the disease that were not the physical signs she could see, so a lot of my inner problems went unsolved or were diagnosed as 'behavioural problems' and treated wrongly."[44]

Because of the attention being paid to the individual affected by the disease, younger brothers or sisters in the household may experience feelings of anxiety or isolation. Older family members such as the parents of the patient may require the support of therapists, social workers, or counselors to help them adapt to the changes that caring for the patient may bring about. Experts say that it is important that each member of the household receives the care and support he or she needs, not just the person who contracted the disease.

Contact with Other Survivors

What many survivors find is that talking to someone who has gone through the same experience is often helpful. The Meningitis Trust is just one group that offers a twenty four-hour help line through which such support may be obtained. Recalls one recovering patient after speaking with someone at the help line:

> At first I was a little shy of phoning someone I didn't know but after a few times I felt really at ease. It's great to talk to someone who has been through similar experiences and is further ahead in the process we are beginning to go through. Without the help of the one-to-one contact service that the Meningitis Trust provided, I don't think that my family would be at the stage we are now, and neither would I have met a great friend like Sue."[45]

The Meningitis Research Foundation provides a similar service called befriending, whereby an individual can speak with someone else who has had an experience with meningitis. Joanna, who lost a teenage son to the disease, was put in contact with Jeni, who became a trained befriender after losing a daughter to meningitis. Said Joanna, "Jeni was able to share

We Lost Our Children

Protect Your Children from Meningitis
Please don't wait... Vaccinate!

Each of these women lost a college-age child to meningitis. They now visit high schools to encourage teens to get vaccinated against the disease.

her experience with me, which helped me to understand that my feelings were totally natural, and that allowed me to deal with them. But the biggest single benefit Jeni brought me was light at the end of a very dark tunnel. Befriending has been good for me and I believe it can be good for others too."[46]

Dealing with the aftereffects of meningitis—both psychological and physical—can be as intimidating as overcoming the disease itself. Family members, friends, and those who have been in the same situation can be invaluable sources of strength for patients dealing with this life-changing event.

CHAPTER FIVE

Meningitis and the Future

Despite the advances that public health authorities in nations around the world made in vaccinating their populations against meningitis over the past decade or two, significant challenges still exist. The disease in its varied forms remains a substantial threat in many countries. Scientists are working in laboratories around the world to provide hope for the future treatment and control of the disease.

Breaking Through the Blood-Brain Barrier

One challenge researchers are addressing is creating improved vaccines. To this end, scientists are working on gaining a better understanding of the mechanisms involved in the operation of the blood-brain barrier. By doing so, they hope to reach an understanding of how the disease-causing microbes are able to get past this natural obstacle. Kelly Doran of the University of California at San Diego is making progress in unlocking the mystery of how to break through this barrier. Her team of researchers has discovered that certain strains of streptococcal meningitis have more difficulty getting through the barrier than others. It appears that these weaker strains lack a molecule that otherwise protrudes from the bacteria's exterior and penetrates the blood-brain barrier. In effect, this molecule works as a kind of key. To prove their theory, Doran's team in-

72

jected a group of mice with a genetically engineered meningitis strain lacking this key. Ninety percent of the injected rodents survived. Mice injected with a normal strain of the bacteria died within days.

If follow-up studies confirm these results, scientists think it may be possible to come up with a drug or vaccine that can alter the blood-brain barrier, essentially changing the locks. This would effectively eliminate the pathway through which germs that cause meningitis could reach the cerebrospinal fluid and infect a person.

Overcoming Resistance to Antibiotics

One of the reasons scientists continue to search for new vaccines and medications is that in recent times, many bacteria have become resistant to existing antibiotics. The feeling among many in the medical community in the 1980s was that

Like this microbiologist at the U.S. Centers for Disease Control, researchers around the world are investigating the control and treatment of meningitis.

meningitis—indeed, infectious diseases in general—were well on their way to being under control. As far back as 1967, Surgeon General William H. Stewart announced it was "time to close the book on infectious diseases, declare the war against pestilence won, and shift national resources to such chronic problems as cancer and heart disease."[47] Many drug companies began shifting their resources away from creating new antibiotics, turning their research instead toward antiviral and antifungal medicines. Said Keith Bostian, formerly a researcher at the Merck Research Laboratory, "There was a sense that the market and the clinical needs were already pretty well satisfied with existing agents."[48]

Since that time, however, the evolution of bacteria able to resist existing antibiotics—including antibiotics used to fight meningitis—has caused pharmaceutical firms to turn their attention back to the search for new antibiotics able to kill these new strains of bacteria. Reported Michael Lancaster, section chief for antimicrobial resistance in the division of hospital infections at the Centers for Disease Control and Prevention, "Drug resistance is just an increasing problem in essentially every kind of bacterium that causes infection."[49]

Genomic Sequencing

New developments in the production of vaccines are taking place through genomic sequencing. These developments are creating opportunities for identifying new vaccines and improving the safety and efficacy of existing ones. Although the battle has been long and tedious, more and more bacteria, viruses, yeasts, plants, and animals now have fully sequenced genomes. What this means is that these organisms' complete set of genetic building blocks are now known.

The very first free-living organism to have its genome completely sequenced was *Haemophilus influenzae*, a bacterium that causes one form of meningitis. In 2000, researchers announced the sequencing of all the genes of two common strains of *Neisseria meningitidis*. These data helped scientists identify bacterial proteins that might eventually lead to a vaccine for one of those strains.

In 2005 a medical team in Alaska sets off to investigate an outbreak of *Haemophilus influenzae* meningitis.

Says professor Brian Spratt, Deputy Director of the Wellcome Trust Centre for the Epidemiology of Infectious Disease at the University of Oxford in England, "Comparison of the different meningococcal genomes may reveal genes that distinguish hypervirulent strains from the majority which are rarely associated with disease and help us understand the reasons for such increased virulence [harmfulness or deadliness]."[50] Explains researcher Hervé Tettelin of the Institute for Genomic Research in Rockville, Maryland, "If you better understand how a species achieves virulence, you can better tackle them before they cause disease." Genomic sequencing is the first step in reaching that understanding. "Only when you have the whole genome sequence," continues Tettelin, "do you have all the pieces of the puzzle."[51]

Pharmacogenomics

In addition to playing a role in the production of new vaccines, genomic sequencing might also prove beneficial in another way. Every year, thousands of people, including some being treated

Intranasal Vaccines

It is likely that natural immunity to group B meningococcal bacteria develops following momentary contact between the immune system and the bacteria at the back of the nose and throat. A project at the University of Bristol is examining how this works. Researchers are using a new device to administer an experimental group B vaccine through the nose. It is hoped that such a vaccine, administered in this manner, will mimic the natural immunization process, provide a solution to the disease, and help with the design of new vaccines. Researchers believe a vaccine delivered in this way will also reduce the likelihood of adverse effects.

Computer artwork depicts how an intranasal spray delivers drugs to the brain.

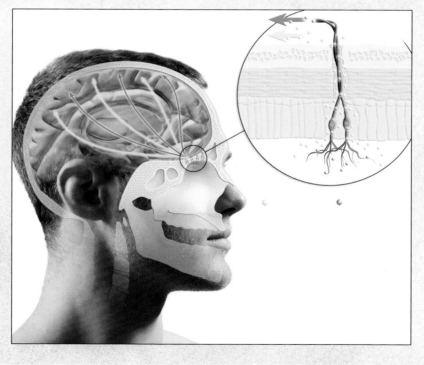

for meningitis, die from adverse drug reactions. Currently, there is no simple way of knowing whether a person will have such a negative response or will respond well or not at all to a particular drug. Because of this, pharmaceutical companies must develop drugs to which the average person will respond.

The manner in which a patient responds to a drug is determined by that individual's genetic makeup. Without knowing all the genes involved, it was not possible to predict how a person would respond. The science that examines these inherited variations and explores how they can be used to predict whether a person will have a good response to a drug, a bad response, or no response at all is called pharmacogenomics.

In order to do this, a person's DNA must be examined for the presence of certain variations. The traditional gene sequencing technology that can do this is very slow and costly. DNA microarrays are a new technology that enables this process to be done more quickly and affordably. As the technology develops further, such screening to determine a response to a drug will become commonplace. The ability to gauge a patient's reaction to a drug before it is prescribed should reduce the number of adverse drug reactions significantly and increase the confidence with which physicians can prescribe the medication. Since the probability of successful therapy would be increased, this, in turn, should lower the cost of health care even as it saves lives.

Vaccines in the Meningitis Belt

For all the excitement over improving the treatment of meningitis, many experts say the key is to improve access to existing vaccines. These experts note that the use of vaccines has drastically cut down the number of cases of bacterial meningitis in the United States since the mid-1980s. The disease remains a serious problem, however, in parts of the world where such programs have not—or cannot—be implemented. The highest rate of meningococcal disease can be found in the dry savannah parts of the Sahel region of sub-Saharan Africa. Known as the "meningitis belt," this area stretches from Ethiopia in the east to Senegal in the west. It touches eighteen countries and

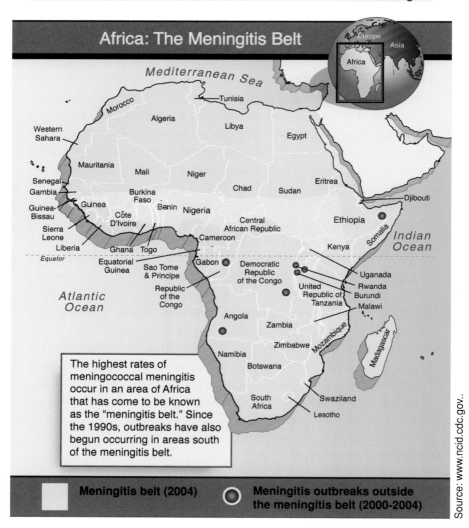

Africa: The Meningitis Belt

The highest rates of meningococcal meningitis occur in an area of Africa that has come to be known as the "meningitis belt." Since the 1990s, outbreaks have also begun occurring in areas south of the meningitis belt.

Meningitis belt (2004)

Meningitis outbreaks outside the meningitis belt (2000-2004)

Source: www.ncid.cdc.gov..

more than 350 million people. Since the mid-1990s, the meningitis belt appears to be extending even farther south.

Although epidemics of meningitis occur worldwide, over the past fifty years epidemics of the meningococcal variety of the disease have struck the countries of the meningitis belt in Africa with regularity. Burkina Faso, Ethiopia, Chad, and Niger have been especially hard-hit. In 2002, Burkina Faso, Ethiopia, and Niger accounted for approximately 65 percent of the cases reported on the entire continent.

During these outbreaks, individual communities have reported rates as high as 1,000 cases per 100,000 persons. Since 1995, more than 700,000 cases and 60,000 deaths have been attributed to the disease. The largest recorded outbreak in history occurred in 1996, when more than 250,000 cases and 25,000 deaths were reported. Young children have the highest rate of infection during normal periods, but older children, teenagers, and young adults are also affected during epidemics.

Whether mass vaccination can effectively prevent meningitis depends on the strain of bacteria that is involved. Most of the major epidemics have been caused by serogroup A, which can be controlled to some degree through the use of a readily available vaccine. In recent years, however, serogroup W135 emerged in a sizable outbreak in Burkina Faso. An affordable vaccine for W135 is far less accessible, so it is questionable whether preventive steps could have been taken.

Furthermore, some factors that determine the seriousness of an outbreak are almost impossible to control. The highest disease morbidity rate (rate of disease incidence) occurs during the dry season. At that time, the dry climate and crowded living conditions favor increased transmission of the disease. Explains Isabelle Jeanne of the Centre de Recherche Médicale et Sanitaire in Niger: "The dryness and dust does not spread the bacteria directly. Instead it seems as though the irritation caused to local inhabitants' mucus [sic] membranes renders them more vulnerable to bacterial infection."[52]

A New Approach

Over the past few decades, the approach taken by public health officials has focused on early detection of the disease and mass vaccination of the at-risk population with polysaccharide vaccines (those produced from the purified sugar coating of bacteria that cause infection). These vaccines meet the needs of industrialized nations, where outbreaks of meningitis tend to be small.

These vaccines do not, however, provide long-lasting protection, and they are ineffective in very young children. As a result, individuals do not develop lasting immunity and must be revaccinated every three to five years. Repeated vaccination of such a large target group is not easily implemented in Africa, particularly, because the costs involved make vaccines unaffordable to the largely poor nations there.

In order to circumvent the limitations of this approach in the meningitis belt, officials of the Meningitis Vaccine Project devised a plan calling for a conjugate meningococcal vaccine. Such vaccines—created by taking a mild antigen and binding it to a stronger one to force the body's immune system to recognize it and develop antibodies—have been used to fight meningococcal disease with great success. Says U.S. Food and Drug Administration scientist Carl E. Frasch, "Because conjugate vaccines can induce immunonologic memory it can result in a long-lasting protection (in contrast to polysaccharide vaccines). It can also be used in young infants."[53]

In 2000 a panel of experts was commissioned by the World Health Organization to assess the feasibility of the project. The panel found that large pharmaceutical firms would not be willing to produce the vaccine for less than one dollar per dose, a price most nations in the meningitis belt would be unable to afford.

Turning to India

To surmount this obstacle, the Meningitis Vaccine Project decided to work with a pharmaceutical company in a country where the vaccine could be made at a much lower cost. The firm selected was the Serum Institute of India. Says Frasch, "In order to assure a low-priced, high quality vaccine we had chosen this highly respected developing country manufacturer."[54] India's large, well-trained workforce demands far lower wages even as workers produce high-quality drugs in state-of-the-art facilities.

The vaccine was then manufactured, tested, and stored in India. The result is a new, affordable conjugate meningitis vaccine A (Men A). According to the World Health Organization, the venture will produce 25 million doses of the vaccine per year at a cost as low as forty cents per dose.

Dr. Suresh Jadhav, executive director of the Serum Institute of India, believes this new approach will be beneficial in the fight against disease. Says Jadhav: "The success of Men A will indeed map the way to new drugs and vaccines. It will help basic research from the universities reach the poor."[55]

Although this vaccine should help bring the disease under control, it likely will not eradicate it in the immediate future. Mass immunization in that region of Africa would be needed on a scale that is not yet possible. Presently, then, the vaccine is targeted for the areas most likely to be affected by the disease. This presents another problem.

The Meningitis Forecasting for Africa Project

Typically, meningitis outbreaks occur in seven-to-fourteen-year cycles. Although meningococcal meningitis is a cyclical disease, it is still impossible to know for sure where or when an outbreak will occur. An epidemic might strike one region one year but leave it almost completely untouched the next. Previously unaffected areas have also been struck by the disease.

For years, scientists have known that epidemics in Africa are associated with very dry conditions. In 1995 Liverpool University scientists confirmed that meningitis does not strike when the absolute humidity of the air remains above 10 grams per cubic meter (0.35 oz. per cubic foot) throughout the year. Says Dr. Andy Morse: "This may sound like an academic discovery, but it had important implications. If we could show that climate affects not only where epidemics occur but also when, it should be possible to identify which people to protect from the disease before it strikes."[56]

Based on these findings, the Meningitis Forecasting for Africa Project was born in 1998. The first stage of the project, directed by Dr. Madeleine Thomson, involved collecting meteorological data relevant to the transmission of the disease. The next step was to uncover relationships between the environment and the location of the epidemics. The factors deemed most relevant were land cover type and seasonal absolute humidity, with population density, soil type, and seasonal dust patterns also significant. Explains Dr. Luis Cuevas of the Liverpool School of Tropical Medicine:

The Meningitis Vaccine Project

The Meningitis Vaccine Project (MVP) is a partnership between the World Health Organization and the Program for Appropriate Technology in Health. It was created in 2001 with core funding coming from a $70 million grant from the Bill and Melinda Gates Foundation. The MVP's mission, as stated on its Web site, is "to eliminate meningitis as a public health problem in sub-Saharan Africa through the development, testing, introduction, and widespread use of conjugate meningococcal vaccines."

In order to fulfill this mission, the site lists the group's six objectives:

- To develop meningococcal conjugate vaccines that are appropriate for use in Africa

- To create pathways for the licensure of vaccines

- To assure production in sufficient volume at a price that facilitates wide use in Africa

- To monitor the effectiveness and safety of the vaccines in controlled clinical trials

- To investigate innovative ways to finance the procurement of vaccines through local, country, and other global programs

- To introduce the vaccines through mass and routine immunization in synergy with other public health programs."

Realizing the importance of understanding the needs and perspectives of the individual countries, the MVP does not simply make vaccines available, but rather works closely with African public health officials to make decisions and implement strategies that are most likely to be effective, while taking into account the financial restraints of the nations involved.

A. Meningitis Vaccine Project, "Mission." www.meningvax.org/mission.htm.

The Meningitis Forecasting for Africa Project predicts the time and location of epidemics, enabling people like this woman to be vaccinated prior to an outbreak.

We developed a risk map showing where epidemics of meningitis are most likely to occur. . . . We then created models capable of predicting when an epidemic was likely to occur in a particular area. . . . Preliminary results suggest that dusty and dry conditions early in the meningitis season followed by the later arrival of the rainy season may signal an increase in cases.[57]

The model was run in predictive mode for the first time in 2002. Reports Cuevas, "The results for Niger were encouraging, but those for Burkina Faso were disappointing—until we discovered a new strain of the bacterium had emerged [W135], wreaking havoc on a population which had no immunity to it."[58]

The research team looks to improve forecasting in the future by factoring in the roles of natural immunity development, the use of vaccines, and the introduction of new bacterial strains in a region. A reliable method for predicting where outbreaks may occur, together with a better understanding of how meningitis attacks the body and advances in producing medications to help treat and prevent the disease, give increased hope to the millions of people around the world who are still susceptible to the ravages of this dreaded disease.

Notes

Introduction: A Global Threat

1. Quoted in Theresa Defino, "New Vaccines Aim to Minimize Meningitis," *WebMD*, June 6, 2000. http://my.webmd.com/content/Article/25/1728_58224_htm.
2. Quoted in *Nova*, "Killer Disease on Campus," September 3, 2002. www.pbs.org/wghb/nova/transcripts/2909_mening git.html.
3. Quoted in *Nova*, "Killer Disease on Campus."
4. Quoted in Lisa Collier Cool, "Danger in the Dorm," *Family Circle*, February 17, 2004, pp. 12–16.

Chapter 1: What Is Meningitis?

5. Quoted in David Birnbaum, "Antimicrobial Resistance: A Deadly Burden No Country Can Afford to Ignore," Canadian Committee on Antibiotic Research. www.ccar-ccra.com/english/word/FinalReport2.doc.
6. Quoted in Allan R. Tunkel, *Bacterial Meningitis*. Philadelphia: Lippincott Williams & Wilkins, 2001, p. 4.
7. Quoted in Scott LaFee, "Flow Stopper," *San Diego Union-Tribune*, October 1, 2003.
8. Quoted in Randy Dotinga, "Researchers Unlock Meningitis' Secrets," *MedicineNet*, September 2, 2005.
9. *Nova*, "Killer Disease on Campus."
10. *Nova*, "Killer Disease on Campus."
11. Dr. Greene, "Haemophilus influenzae." www.drgreene.com.
12. Quoted in *Touching Lives*, "Countering the Deadly Threat of Meningitis," December 2003.
13. Quoted in *Nova*, "Killer Disease on Campus."
14. Quoted in Linda A. Johnson, "Tracking a Killer," *South-Coast Today*, February 24, 1998. www.s-t.com/daily/02-98/02-24-98/c01he098.htm.

Chapter 2: A Medical Emergency

15. Quoted in Karl Lydersen, "Students Should Know Meningitis Symptoms," *Daily Wildcat*, Northwestern University. www.stp.uh.edu/vol61/107/4a.html.
16. Quoted in Mike Burns, "New Symptoms Can Aid Early Diagnosis of Meningitis: Study," *Earthtimes*, January 12, 2006. www.earthtimes.org/articles/show/4982.html.
17. Quoted in Surgery Door: Diseases in Depth, "Case Histories." www.surgerydoor.co.uk.
18. Quoted in *Lancashire Evening Telegraph*, "Living with Meningitis," September 29, 2000.
19. Quoted in *Lancashire Evening Telegraph*, "Living with Meningitis."
20. James G. Zimmerly, "Medical Legal Issues in the Evaluation of the Febrile Pediatric Patient," *Legal Medicine 1999*, May 1, 1999. www.afip.org/Departments/legalmed/openfile99/toc99.html.
21. Quoted in Surgery Door: Diseases in Depth, "Case Histories."
22. Quoted in Meningitis Trust, "Don't Wait for a Rash, Warns Meningitis Charity," January 7, 2003. http://test.epcdirect.co.uk/meningitis/media/media_releases.php.
23. Nancy Appleton, "Sugar Addiction." www.whale.to/w/appleton3.html.
24. Carina A. Rodriguez, and Elaine I. Tuomanen, "Bacterial Meningitis," *Current Treatment Options in Infectious Diseases*, 2000.

Chapter 3: Preventing Meningitis

25. Quoted in Health 24, "Genetics Tied to Meningitis." www.health24.com/medical/Condition_centres/777-792-1987-1998,21985.asp.
26. Quoted in BBC News, "Kissing Increases Meningitis Risk," September 3, 1998. http://news.bbc.co.uk/1/hi/health/163992.stm.
27. Quoted in *Nova*, "Killer Disease on Campus."
28. Quoted in Luther College, "Meningococcal Meningitis Vaccine." http://health.luther.edu/health_and_wellness/meningitis.html.

29. Quoted in Irene S. Levine, "This Disease Isn't Rare Enough for Me," *Health*, July/August 2004.

Chapter 4: A Lifetime of Consequences

30. Quoted in Cool, "Danger in the Dorm."
31. Quoted in "After Effects," Meningitis Trust. www.meningitis-trust.org.
32. Sandra Stuart, "Sandra's Story," Meningitis Research Foundation of Canada. www.meningitis.ca/my_story/sandra.asp.
33. Quoted in Everybody, "Meningitis—Recovery." www.everybody.co.nz/page-7b430f97-3bc8-4def-b480-c444e3da7e9a.aspx.
34. Quoted in Everybody, "Meningitis—Recovery."
35. Ved Mehta, "Sightless in a Sighted World," Ved Mehta.com. www.vedmehta.com.
36. Quoted in Cool, "Danger in the Dorm."
37. Quoted in Cool, "Danger in the Dorm."
38. Quoted in Lois Ann Demko, "I Lost My Limbs," *Seventeen*, October 2004.
39. Quoted in Demko, "I Lost My Limbs."
40. Quoted in Surgery Door: Diseases in Depth, "Case Histories."
41. Quoted in *Time*, "Second Time Around," July 9, 1951.
42. Quoted in Meningitis Trust, "After Meningitis." www.meningitis-trust.org/disease_info/after_meningitisphp?category=22&section2&sub=245.
43. Quoted in Meningitis Research Foundation of Canada. www.meningitis.ca.
44. Gaynor W. Baker, "Gaynor Baker," Meningitis Research Foundation of Canada. www.meningitis.ca/my_story/gaynor.asp.
45. Quoted in Meningitis Trust, "One-to-One." www.meningitis-trust.org.
46. Quoted in Meningitis Research Foundation. www.meningitis.org.

Chapter 5: Meningitis and the Future

47. Quoted in Marc Lallanilla, "As New Strains of Bacteria Threaten Public Health, the Government and the Drug

Industry Struggle to Keep Up," ABC News, November 11, 2004. abcnews.go.com/Health/print?id=241755.

48. Quoted in Mary Knudson, "Battling Bacterial Resistance," *Technology Review*, January/February 1998. www.tech nologyreview.com/articles/98/01/knudson0198.0.asp.

49. Quoted in Knudson, "Battling Bacterial Resistance."

50. Quoted in Oxford University *Gazette*, "Genome Sequence of Epidemic Meningitis Revealed," May 4, 2000. www.ox. ac.uk/gazette/1999-00/weeky/040500/news/story_4.htm.

51. Quoted in Leslie Pray, "Microbes Rule," *Scientist*, March 2003.

52. Quoted in Live Science, "Dust Storms May Start Epidemics." www.livescience.com/imageoftheday/siod_050511.html.

53. Quoted in Dr. Sanjit Bagchi, "New Meningitis Vaccine in the Pipeline," *Science in Africa*, July 2004. www.scien-ceinafrica.com.za/2004/july/meningitis.htm.

54. Quoted in Bagchi, "New Meningitis Vaccine in the Pipeline."

55. Quoted in Bagchi, "New Meningitis Vaccine in the Pipeline."

56. Quoted in Research Intelligence, "Meningitis: Forecasting Why, Where and When," February 3, 2003. www.liv.ac.uk/researchintelligence/html/current/11.html.

57. Quoted in Research Intelligence, "Meningitis."

58. Quoted in Research Intelligence, "Meningitis."

Glossary

agent: A factor, such as an organism, whose presence is essential for the occurrence of a disease.

antibiotic: A drug that kills bacteria and other germs.

antibody: A substance produced by the immune system used to fight disease.

antigen: A foreign substance in the body capable of causing disease.

arachnoid: The middle layer of the meninges.

bacteria: Microscopic, single-celled organisms.

blood-brain barrier: The barrier consisting of blood vessels and nerves that protects the brain from harmful chemicals and organisms.

carriage: The act or process of transporting or carrying a disease agent.

central nervous system: The brain and spinal cord.

cerebrospinal fluid: The clear fluid that bathes and protects the brain and spinal cord.

coccus: A spherical-shaped bacterial cell.

contagious: Easily spread from one person to another.

diagnosis: The identification of a disease from its signs and symptoms.

dura mater: The outermost layer of the meninges.

encephalitis: An inflammation of the brain caused by a viral infection.

endemic: Native to a certain region.

endotoxins: Poisons found in the cell walls of certain bacteria.

enterovirus: A virus that infects the gastrointestinal tract.

epidemic: A widespread outbreak of an infectious disease.

epilepsy: A central nervous system disorder characterized by recurrent, unprovoked seizures.

exotoxins: Poisonous bacterial secretions that leave the cell and enter the environment around the cell.

fever: A rise in body temperature that is frequently a symptom of infection.

hemorrhaging: heavy bleeding.

herd immunity: The resistance of a group to an infectious agent based on the resistance to infection of a high proportion of individuals in the group.

high-risk group: A group with a greater-than-average likelihood of contracting a disease.

immune system: The system of the body that defends it against infection, disease, and foreign organisms.

immunity: Protection against a disease.

infection: An invasion of the body by a disease organism.

inflammation: A bodily response to infection or irritation characterized by pain, swelling, redness, and heat.

meninges: The membranes that surround the brain and spinal cord.

meningitis: An infection or inflammation of the meninges.

microbes: Microscopic organisms, such as bacteria, protozoa, viruses, and fungi.

morbidity: The number of people who contract a disease.

mortality: The death rate from a disease.

mucous membranes: Moist tissues that line the digestive, genitourinary, and respiratory tracts.

outbreak: A sudden appearance of many cases of a disease in a particular area.

paralysis: The inability to move a part of the body.

pathogen: An organism that causes disease in another organism.

pia mater: The innermost layer of the meninges.

pneumonia: An infection of the respiratory system that causes inflammation and fluid buildup in the lungs.

polysaccharide vaccine: A vaccine composed of long chains of sugar molecules.

purpuric rash: A dark red- or purple-colored rash.

septicemia: A serious infection caused by pathogenic microorganisms in the blood.

sign: A condition of a disease that can be seen or measured.

spinal cord: The column of nervous tissue that forms the central pathway of a vertebrate's nervous system.

symptom: A subjective condition of a disease that a patient reports.

vaccine: A substance that activates a person's immune system without causing the actual disease.

virus: An infectious microorganism that contains genetic material but does not contain the other components typically found in cells.

Organizations to Contact

Meningitis Foundation of America
6610 Shadeland Station, Suite 200
Indianapolis, IN 46220
(800) 668-1129
(317) 595-6395
fax: (317) 595-6370
www.musa.org

A nonprofit organization established to help support meningitis sufferers and their families; to provide information to educate everyone about meningitis so that its early diagnosis and treatment will save lives; and to provide medical personnel with information to help them understand and treat the disease.

Meningitis Research Foundation
Midland Way, Thornbury
Bristol BS35 2BS UK
+44 1454 281811
fax: +44 01454 281094
www.meningitis.org

A charity that funds research to prevent meningitis and septicemia and to improve victims' survival rates and outcomes. The foundation promotes education and awareness to reduce death and disability from the disease and gives support to those affected.

National Center for Infectious Diseases
Centers for Disease Control and Prevention
1600 Clifton Rd.
Atlanta, GA 30333
(404) 639-3534
(800) 311-3435

www.cdc.gov/ncidod

One of the thirteen major operating components of the U.S. Department of Health and Human Services, which is the principal agency in the United States government for protecting the health and safety of all Americans and for providing essential human services, especially for those people who are least able to help themselves.

National Institute of Allergy and Infectious Diseases (NIAID) National Institutes of Health
6610 Rockledge Dr., MSC 6612
Bethesda, MD 20892-6612
(301) 496-5717
www.niaid.nih.gov

NIAID conducts and supports basic and applied research to better understand, treat, and ultimately prevent infectious, immunologic, and allergic diseases.

National Meningitis Association
22910 Chestnut Rd.
Lexington Park, MD 20653
(866) FONE-NMA (366-3662)
fax: (877) 703-6096
www.nmaus.org

A nonprofit organization founded by five parents whose children died or suffered long-term disabilities from meningococcal meningitis. Its mission is to educate families, medical professionals, and others about bacterial meningitis and prevention approaches to the disease.

For Further Reading

Books

Keith Cartwright, ed., *Meningococcal Disease*. New York: Wiley, 1995. A compilation of information on all aspects of meningococcal disease.

Karen L. Roos, *Meningitis: 100 Maxims*. London: Edward Arnold, 1996. This volume in the 100 Maxims in Neurology series offers one hundred principles to help practitioners in the diagnosis and treatment of the disease.

Brian R. Shmaefsky, *Deadly Diseases and Epidemics: Meningitis*. Philadelphia: Chelsea House, 2005. This volume in the Deadly Diseases and Epidemics series explores the various forms, symptoms, and treatments of meningitis.

Lewis Thomas, *The Youngest Science: Notes of a Medicine Watcher*. New York: Viking, 1983. A doctor's account of his life in medicine and an inquiry into what medicine is all about.

Allan R. Tunkel, *Bacterial Meningitis*. Philadelphia: Lippincott Williams & Wilkins, 2001. Clinically oriented work covering every aspect of bacterial meningitis.

Periodicals

Lisa Collier Cool, "Danger in the Dorm," *Family Circle*, February 17, 2004.

Lois Ann Demko, "I Lost My Limbs," *Seventeen*, October 2004.

Lancashire Evening Telegraph (UK), "Living with Meningitis," September 29, 2000.

Irene S. Levine, "This Disease Isn't Rare Enough for Me," *Health*, July/August 2004.

Kara G. Morrison, "Meningitis: A Swift, Merciless, Mysterious Killer," *Detroit News*, September 18, 2002.

Carina A. Rodriguez and Elaine I. Tuomanen, "Bacterial Meningitis," *Current Treatment Options in Infectious Diseases*, 2000.

Touching Lives, "Countering the Deadly Threat of Meningitis," December 2003.

Internet Sources

Gaynor W. Baker, "Gaynor Baker," Meningitis Research Foundation of Canada. www.meningitis.ca/my_story/gaynor.asp.

Dr. Greene, "Bacterial Meningitis." www.drgreene.com/21_786. html.

Dr. Greene, "*Haemophilus Influenzae.*" www.drgreene.com/ body.cfm?id=21&action=detail&ref=1102.

Everybody, "Meningitis—Recovery." www.everybody.co.nz/ page-7b430f97-3bc8-4def-b480-c444e3da7e9a.aspx.

Linda A. Johnson, "Tracking a Killer," *SouthCoast Today*, February 24, 1998. www.s-t.com/daily/02-98/02-24 98/c01he098. htm.

Meningitis Trust, "After Meningitis." www.meningitistrust.org/ disease_info/after_meningitis.php?category=2z&section=2& sub=245.

Sandra Stuart, "Sandra's Story," Meningitis Research Foundation of Canada. www.meningitis.ca/my_story/sandra.asp.

Surgery Door: Diseases in Depth, "Case Histories." www. surgerydoor.co.uk.

This Is Local London, "Living with Meningitis," August 10, 2000. www.thisislocallondon.co.uk/misc/print.php?artid= 106210.

John Travis, "Two Meningitis Bacteria Yield Genomes," *Science News Online*, February 19, 2000. www.sciencenews. org.

Web Sites

KidsHealth (http://kidshealth.org). Created by the Nemours Foundation's Center for Children's Health Media, KidsHealth is the largest site on the Web providing doctor-approved health information about children from before birth through adolescence.

Meningitis Angels (www.meningitis-angels.org). This nonprofit organization composed of survivors and families of meningitis victims endeavors to educate the public on bacterial meningitis and methods of prevention.

Meningitis Vaccine Project (www.meningvax.org). A partnership between the World Health Organization and the Program for Appropriate Technology in Health, the Meningitis Vaccine Project's goal is to eliminate epidemic meningitis as a public health problem in sub-Saharan Africa.

Moms on Meningitis (http://moms.nmaus.org). Formed by the National Meningitis Association, Moms on Meningitis is a coalition of mothers whose children have been affected by meningitis.

Videos

Don't Catch the Killer, VHS. Produced by Australia Media One, 2003. This video recounts the experiences of six young adults who have battled meningitis and relates their candid advice about the disease.

Fighting Meningococcal Disease, VHS. Produced by Australia Media One, 2002. This comprehensive guide explains everything a person should know about the recognition, treatment, and prevention of meningococcal disease.

Killer Disease on Campus: Meningitis, VHS. Produced by WGBH Boston, 2002. *Nova* explores various aspects of meningitis, including its warning signs, how doctors are struggling to control outbreaks, and what can be done to prevent children and college students from contracting the deadly disease.

Index

adults
  meningitis in, 24, 50-51
Africa, sub-Saharan, 10,
    46–47
  forecasting outbreaks in,
    81–84
  vaccination in, 77–79
  see also meningitis belt
amputation, 58, 63, 65
antibiotics, 41–43
  for prevention of
    meningitis, 53–54
  resistance to, 54, 73-74
Appleton, Nancy, 43
arachnoid, 17

bacteria, 20
bacterial meningitis, 10, 20
  world wide, 11
bereavement, 68
blindness, 62
blood-brain barrier, 19, 72
  breakdown of, 22
  penetrating, 42, 43
Bostian, Keith, 74
brain
  inflammation of, 17–18, 41
  see also blood-brain barrier
British Medical Journal, 54
Brudzinski's sign, 32

central nervous system, 13

  see also brain
chemoprophylaxis, 53–54
chicken pox virus, 28
children, 50, 51
college campuses
  immunizations on, 56–57
  meningitis in, 11
    prevalence of, 12
    risks for, 48
computerized tomography
  (CT scan), 39
Cryptococcal neoformans, 29,
  53
Cuevas, Luis, 81, 83
*Current treatment Options
  in Infectious Diseases*
  (journal), 44

Danielson, L., 16
death rates
  from bacterial
    meningitis,11, 12
Doran, Kelly, 19, 72
Dr.Greene.com, 25
dura mater, 17

Elkington, Steve, 67
encephalitis, meningitis vs., 16
endotoxins, effects of, 23–24
enteroviruses, 28
Escherichia coli (E. coli), 27,
  51

98

Picture Credits

About the Author

John F. Grabowski is a native of Brooklyn, New York. He holds a bachelor's degree in psychology from City College of New York and a master's degree in educational psychology from Teachers College, Columbia University. He has been a teacher for thirty-five years, as well as a freelance writer, specializing in the fields of sports, education, and comedy. His body of published works includes forty-nine books; a nationally syndicated sports column; consultation on several math textbooks; articles for newspapers, magazines, and the programs of professional sports teams; and comedy material sold to Jay Leno, Joan Rivers, Yakov Smirnoff, and numerous other comics. He and his wife, Patricia, live in Staten Island with their daughter, Elizabeth.